THE BASTARD
The Cry of the Damned

THE BASTARD

The Cry of the Damned

G. D. Dawson

The Book Guild Ltd

Sussex, England

The Book Guild Ltd
25 High Street
Lewes, Sussex

First published 1990
© G. D. Dawson 1990
Set in Baskerville
Typeset by Hawks Phototypesetters Ltd
Copthorne, West Sussex
Printed in Great Britain by
Antony Rowe Ltd
Chippenham, Wiltshire

British Library Cataloguing in Publication Data
Dawson, G. D. (Geoffrey Dunstan)
    The bastard: the cry of the damned.
    1. Great Britain. Social life. 1945 — Biographies
    I. Title
941.085092

ISBN 0 86332 474 6

CONTENTS

When the horizon no longer separates the heavens from the earth, then know you truly from where you cometh. If tears could fall like autumn leaves, then I have wept a forest.

G.D.D. 1988

Introduction

This book has been written after much thought was taken whether or not to undertake such a task.

I have written the book not, as many a clever psychiatrist would say, to appease some inner urge or need to psychoanalyse myself, but to tell the story of my childhood once and for all, to all those doubting Thomas's who smugly sneer behind their hands at such a story, which is frankly to them somewhat unbelievable.

In the verbal telling of this story, I have been looked upon like someone who has come from a different planet. To those who have felt superior to me, I have been likened to a Walter Mitty character. Others have remarked on how lucky I am to still be mentally normal after such experiences, implying that they think me nowhere near normal. Others have frankly accused me of being a liar, judging my life against their own experiences.

But, to the less than a handful of people who have believed me, I thank you for the courage and support you have steadfastly given me during the time I have known you.

I have tried to lay out the facts of my early life as closely to the truth as my memory will allow. Where memory has failed, I have taken a small dose of literary licence.

If anyone wishes to challenge the facts which are laid down, let them do so; but first they had better bow their heads in abject shame for being involved in what can only be described as a disgraceful act against another human being.

I bear no hatred against those who were responsible for what was done to me; that light has long been burnt out. I can only feel sorry for them that they knew no better.

There is one person to whom I must pay homage.

Miss Dianne Harriss Reed.

She was a young lady of not more than about twenty years of age when I knew her at the beginning of the Eighties. She came to me from England, and spent two weeks typing out my very first manuscript and effort as a writer. She patiently sorted out my literary chaos and transformed it into a readable, if not acceptable form. From her efforts I was able to realise I could, if I worked hard, one day reach the goal of being a writer.

Within three weeks of her leaving me and returning to England, she was brutally murdered by a sex maniac in a London nurses' home.

I was never informed of these events until many weeks later, too late, I felt, to telephone her family and console them.

I now wish to take this opportunity of thanking the memory of this young lady for her selfless efforts to help me, and say that without her help at the beginning I would probably have given up the idea of being a writer a long time ago. The book she was working on was this one.

The contents of this book are true, no matter how embarrassing they may be for me to relate. In telling this story I absolve the publisher of any responsibility for the contents. And finally I hope this book will silence those who feel a need to belittle me.

Geoffrey Dunstan Dawson
June 1988.

I

The Second World War has been over less than six months, and yet there is still a siege mentality among the people who are trying hard to adjust to the fact that the seven year war is really at an end. The Royal Air Force Flight Lieutenant Geoffrey Dunstan . . . tall, slim, and looking resplendent in his uniform, still has to pick his way carefully among the bombing rubble as he makes his way to the rendezvous with the young woman.

He knows he should never be keeping this appointment with the small, slim, dark-haired young woman. As a married man of 46 years old, he knows he is taking a very unfair advantage of the 22-year-old woman; but his vanity and ego have taken him far beyond the point where he cares anymore.

He knows the young woman is attracted to him, after all, she is easy to impress with his war stories about bombing missions over Germany. And he realises he can twist the young girl around his little finger, because he knows she has a slight mental backwardness which makes her very trusting.

He knows all this as he makes his way to the rendezvous, and realises there is the slightest element of guilt inside of him as he thinks about the advantage he's taking of Emily Dawson. But then he thinks about her slim young body below his, and his lust replaces any sense of responsibility. A good meal, something to drink, and then the night will end in the bed she occupies in the servants' quarters of his father's house.

He smiles as he thinks about the stories he will tell her, and how he will impress her with the story about his wealthy family.

★   ★   ★   ★

January 9th 1947

The doctor is sweating almost as much as the patient lying on the bed. He looks over the raised and parted legs which are covered with sheets and catches a glimpse of the young woman's face. The lips are held tight together, the eyes look up to the ceiling with a determined effort not to show the inner pain.

He wished the woman would scream out or something, just to relieve her tension, to be able to measure the amount of pain she was in, but all he could see on the pain-contorted face were the two streams of tears running down onto the pillow. He looks down at the swollen womb and sees the movement of the vagina . . . the child is coming.

'Emily . . . Emily . . . it doesn't hurt to scream at the pain, it's normal. Just take a deep breath, open your mouth and let it all out.'

He hears his own muffled voice behind the face mask wondering whether she has heard him. But he knows she has, she has responded to other things he asked her to do.

'All right Emily . . . we'll do it your way.'

He looks to the nursing sister sat next to Emily's head and nods. He sees the woman move behind the patient and take hold of her shoulders. He looks again to the midwife now standing on his right and nods his head to her, the rest of the theatre staff take their response from the doctor.

'All right Emily . . . I want you to take a deep breath and push just a little against the child.'

He hears the breath being drawn and the stomach muscles contract, and suddenly he can see a blue and red crown of a tiny head begin to approach the light of day. Suddenly he fears Emily will press too hard and cause the child to come too fast.

'Good, Emily . . . good . . . take a rest for a moment . . . I can see the child's head now. We are going to do this in three stages . . . head . . . shoulders and then the rest of the body. Now, Emily . . . please listen to what I say and don't push too hard . . . take it slowly and the child will come into this world at it's own speed. Good? . . . Then let's try. Take a deep breath Emily and press . . .'.

He could now see the child's head straining to come out of the womb, and hoped the skin wouldn't rip, then he saw the head come forward. There was an urgency to his voice.

'Rest a moment, Emily . . . take a few deep breaths and rest.'

He moved his fingers inside the womb and felt to see that the umbilical cord wasn't around the child's neck, he withdrew his bloodied fingers when he was satisfied.

'All right Emily . . . this part will hurt, but it will soon be over . . . none of us mind if you scream . . . it could be good for you.'

He quickly looked over the tops of the legs and saw the sweat-stained face rolling from side to side, tears mingling freely with the sweat. The nurse nodded her head and he turned back to the child. He inserted two of his fingers into the womb and slipped then around the childs neck, the palm of the hand supporting the head.

'You can push now Emily, quite hard . . . but only when I tell you. Push!!! . . . a little harder! . . .'

He could see the slim legs shaking with the effort, the stomach violently rising and falling with the strain. Then the child's head was out and the tiny face was cringing against the violent treatment.

'Rest a moment Emily . . . two or three deep breaths . . . then push again . . ..'

The child's shoulders were in the right position to come out, but they were a little wide, the face was contorting as the child fought against the oxygen and the world it was coming into. He knew he would have to be quick.

'All right, Emily . . . Push! . . . and again . . . a little harder! . . .'

The child seemed to be reluctant to move and then suddenly it was on it's way. The operating theatre was filled with one long and single inhuman scream as the child slid out of the womb onto the rubber covered table . . . and then all was silent.

The doctor and the midwife worked quickly to sever the umbilical cord and clear the blood and mucous from the child's face and mouth, then they held it up by it's ankles and smacked the buttocks. The child's mouth opened wide . . . the doctor smacked it again . . . and then suddenly everyone was smiling and talking at the same time when the baby wailed and drew breath.

The details of Geoffrey Dunstan Dawson's birth were registered in the records of Good Hope Hospital, Sutton Coldfield, in the county of Warwickshire that morning. Under the heading reserved for the father's name, there was just a thin line. Under the heading for the address of the parents, the register recorded the following:

Mother, only parent. Living at 1 Vernon Road, home for Unmarried Mothers.

But it was more than a month later before the details of the child's birth were registered with the Government offices assigned to such details . . . by it's mother.

★   ★   ★   ★

April 1948

It was a typical English spring day. But as was normal in the severe Government establishments, the sun was almost forbidden to cast its rays into the grey stone buildings. Heavy mesh curtains were at every window, preventing the life-giving rays from warming the stale air.

Emily Dawson sat on the hard backed chair and looked down at her hands folded in her lap, whilst the stern-faced official looked at her; mercy was a foreign word to him. He was accompanied by the heavy busted matron of the home for unmarried mothers.

'Miss Dawson. I have a doctor's report here, that is so shocking it is unbelievable. It says you are again . . ..'

The man seemed to struggle with his religious conscience but it failed to give him the strength to utter the word 'Pregnant.'

'. . . with child.'

The thick glass spectacles the man wore seemed to sparkle under the permanent electric light which was needed to illuminate the darkened austere office, whilst outside brilliant sunshine filled the air.

The dark wavy-haired head lifted and nodded.

The man's thin lips became thinner, and the matron lifted her heavy bosoms on her forearms as she looked at the Government official in religious horror.

'Miss Dawson! It would seem you have broken every rule of this establishment. How is it possible that a young woman like you, can ... can ... have such little respect for herself. The matron's report says she has had to restict your freedom because you have been seen to respond to a certain male visitor in ... in a familiar way. Good heavens Miss Dawson, here you are, under the kind care and protection of the city council, who have been good enough to give a home to you and your child; and you sit there and tell me you're ... you're ... pregnant!'

The matron again lifted her heavy bosoms on her arms and nodded her head, her small piggy eyes boring into the shameless woman in front of her.

The man bore down on Emily again.

'Do you realise how irresponsible your actions are? No woman in her normal mind would do what you've done. You are now twice with child and not even married. No man will ever want you. And what's even worse is that you have no job! Your last employer, who was good enough to let you stay at his house with the first child, cannot be expected to tolerate looking after a second child ... from one of his servants.'

For a moment there was silence in the room as the two officials waited for the woman to say something, but she sat silent.

'Who is the father?'

She slowly lifted her head and looked at the man.

'It doesn't matter. Anyway ... I've forgotten his name.'

Again she looked down at her hands ... she would never forget his name ... it was a small price to pay for the few moments of happiness she had experienced.

The stern man bore down on her again.

'Miss Dawson. Unless you tell us who this man is, you forfeit any right to ask the Government to help you. Whoever this man is, he has made you ... pregnant. He must be brought to justice, and made to face the consequences of his actions. I want to know who the man is ... I want his name!'

Emily Dawson looked down at her hands in her lap. Slowly, she clasped them together and remembered what had happened when her son had been born. The same man who now sat in front of her, had threatened her with all the known horrors to make her reveal who the father was. But she had refused, even when they had sent her for a psychiatric study, saying that her act of bringing a child into the world whilst not marrying the father, was the act of a lunatic.

'Why must I be married . . . just to have children?'

The Government man nearly choked on her question.

'Why? . . . Why? . . . because, Miss Dawson, somebody has to look after them. It is a father's duty to earn the money to support the family he brings into the world. It's unthinkable for a . . . an unmarried woman to have children. It's against all God's teachings.'

'God never had children.'

The crack of the file being slammed down on the desk drew Emily's attention to the blood-red face of the Government official.

'Miss Dawson. It is my painful duty to inform you, that due to your irrational and anti-social irresponsibility towards yourself and the child you already have, we, that is the City Council of Birmingham, have decided to remove your son Geoffrey Dunstan Dawson to a place of safety until such times as the courts award parental rights over the unfortunate child to the City.

'Secondly, you will go into a hospital for the birth of your second child and will be sterilised immediately after the birth.

'Thirdly, as soon as the second child can be removed from your custody it too will be taken into care by the city council.

'Fourthly. The moment your second child is taken into care, you will be removed to a mental institution for your own safety.'

The silence in the cold dim-lit room became absolute as Emily Dawson looked down at her hands and absorbed her fate. There were no more tears to be shed, they'd been shed long ago. It was her fate, of that she was sure. But why? All she had wanted, was to have her own children.

'Miss Dawson. I'm waiting for an answer. Have you understood what was said to you?'

The dark haired head barely moved in acknowledgement.

'Good. If you will just sign this paper here, saying you have understood everything.'

Listlessly she took the proffered pen and wrote her name out carefully, where the finger indicated she should sign.

The man sat back with a sigh, as if the world was again in

order.

'Miss Dawson. You need not worry about your children. They will receive the finest upbringing and education this city can provide. If you'll go back to your room now, prepare your things and hand over your son to Matron, you will be taken to a hospital this afternoon were you will be comfortable and able to wait out the birth of the second child.

On the 16th of June 1948, Miss Emily Dawson gave birth to a daughter who was called Jean Dawson. In accordance with the decision made by the Birmingham City Council, Miss Emily Dawson was sterilised and incarcerated in Castlebromwich Mental Hospital for the mentally disabled. She was kept there for well over ten years in a closed institution, fed with high potency drugs against her will.

Her daughter Jean, the full blood sister of Geoffrey, was removed into the custody of the city council and later adopted by a family. Neither of the children were ever told of the presence of the other one. Whenever questions were asked by the son Geoffrey as to the whereabouts of his family, he was told quite sternly he had no family and that his parents had died.

★　　　★　　　★　　　★

Geoffrey Dunstan Dawson. 9.1.47

'If you don't learn the rules of this place the easy way . . . then you can learn them the hard way.'

The broad flat hand descended at an incredible speed and struck the head. Stars and an array of colours and black spots appeared in front of the eyes.

Then there was the sensation of flying through the air, coming up short against a wall and experiencing further bursting colours.

Through the mist filling the head, the eyes registered the fact that the man was advancing, the hand drawn back to hit again. The lips of the face pulled back in determination. Instinct to survive made the child roll into a ball to lessen the incessant blows and kicks that rained down on him.

That, is the very first memory I have of my early life, and is something which I'll remember until the day I die. It was my introduction to a world of violence and brutality which I was to discover, is a peculiar characteristic of the English; a race of people who would starve rather than let their animals go hungry, yet thought nothing of beating their children half to death.

This event took place at a local authority nursery for unwanted children. I was already three and a half years old, and at my third nursery. From April 1948 I had been removed from my mother's care and sent to Hawthorne House nursery, where I was to stay until November 1949. Then I was transferred to a nursery called Milton Grange, but the stay there was extremely short, in fact on December 12th 1949 I was transferred to another nursery called Meadway. It was there I was to stay until May 4th 1951, and it was there that my conscience woke to the world around it and had to take cover at the same time.

I can remember I often cried myself to sleep at night, after what I was to discover were the daily beatings that not only myself, but the other boys also received.

I had no concept whatsoever of what the world was about; it seemed I had just appeared from nowhere and that the beatings I was receiving were absolutely normal.

But one thing I was becoming fast aware of were the adults who presented a risk to my safety. I would learn to hide behind cupboards or doors and even under beds when I saw an adult approaching. Though sometimes hiding under the beds brought me on even more savage beating than the one which I'd been trying to avoid.

I quickly learnt that to survive in such a place, I had to keep well clear of the grown ups and always keep a wary eye out for their approach. I can remember well the scramble that took place as soon as an adult had been seen by one of the boys. Boys would fight each other to keep a hiding place to themselves rather than be exposed to the malevolent glare of an adult, which invariably led to a savage beating and then being sent early to bed without anything further to eat for the rest of the day.

I never realised I could actually communicate with the other boys, because talking was often forbidden. But somehow

I learnt from the other boys what sort of place I was in.

I can remember sitting behind some dustbins with another boy who had been in the nursery for what seemed an eternity. He was about two years older than myself, and was keeping a very wary eye out for the adults whom I was learning were called "Screws" a slang word for a jailer.

'It can take a long time to find parents who'll take you.'

'Parents . . . what are parents?'

'That's . . . well . . . it's grown ups who want children.'

'Do you get beaten often . . . by these . . . adults?'

'Ummm . . . I don't really know. There's one boy who was brought back by his grown ups and he said he'd been beaten all day. In fact it was so bad, they had to put him in hospital. The grown ups said he'd had an accident . . ..'

'How . . . well . . . what do you have to do to get adults?'

'The adults come once a month and have a look at us. That's the day when we are dressed in clean clothes and made to walk around in front of the adults who are interested in taking one of us.'

'What do you have to do to get adults? . . . you know . . . how do you get picked.

The shoulders just shrugged.

'Don't know.'

There were long periods of silence, it was such a lot to take in.

'What's it like?'

'What's what like.'

'You know . . . with the adults . . . where do they take you to . . . what's it like there?'

Again the shoulders were shrugged.

'I don't know. It's not very often one of the boys is brought back. They're usually put into a different nursery, so we can't find out what it's like.'

A sudden wind blew across the yard and covered us in dust. It didn't seem to worry the other boy, so I decided I shouldn't worry about it either.

'Have you ever been outside the gates?'

I nodded my head in the direction of the huge wrought iron gates that seemed to protect us from unknown dangers. His eyes followed my gaze and he seemed to reflect sometime upon the answer.

'I was out there once, but I can't remember much about it. There's lots of people out there, all moving along without really seeing you. If you weren't careful you could easily get knocked down, then somebody would start screaming at you.'

'Will I become an adult?'

'I don't know . . . well . . . I suppose we all become adults.'

'Why are they always hitting us?'

Again the shoulders shrugged.

'I don't know . . . it's . . . I don't know.'

'Will I have to do it when I'm an adult? . . . hit the children.'

'Everybody has to do it. Have you ever seen an adult who doesn't beat children?'

I can remember sitting back and resting my head against the wall, I was scared, really scared. I was scared I wouldn't learn all that had to be learnt to be able to beat the children around me. It seemed there was so much to learn about. I hoped I would learn to be a good child beater.

The playing yard was silent, we carefully looked around the cover of the dustbins to see if there was an adult approaching, but there were none in sight. The warm sun beating down upon us was a pleasure as we sat back against the wall.

'When is the next time the adults come?'

Again he shrugged his shoulders.

'Should be soon . . . haven't seen any around for a long time. When the nursery needs some money, they sell off a few kids. It costs a lot of money when an adult buys us, which is why they don't come too often.'

'Who owns us . . . me . . . who do I belong to . . . that I can be sold to other adults?'

'Don't know . . . I suppose we belong to the people here.'

'Have you been . . . bought?'

'Don't think so . . . I've seen a lot of these adults around . . . but I don't ever seem to get picked.'

My mind was going around in circles. There were questions in my head in the form of feelings, I wasn't quite sure how to say what I wanted to say.

'What . . . er . . . what happens when you get picked?' The silence seemed to go on forever before he answered.

'Try not to get picked. When they tell you to walk around, get as dirty as possible as fast as possible. Walk around with your mouth hanging open. Look as untidy as you can.'

'Why do you have to let your mouth hang open?'

'Don't know . . . but it's one of the secrets here. Everybody does it. The Screws get really crazy and beat the hell out of you after the adults have left, but at least you don't get picked.'

I lay back against the warm wall, trying hard to remember what he'd said. If he'd been able to survive this long without being picked, then he must know what he was talking about. Something about the silence in the yard disturbed me, but also excited me. Perhaps we had been forgotten, after all, there were lots of boys around.

'But what happens if you do get picked?'

I looked and a tremor ran through him.

'You're taken to the place where these people live. Sometimes it's nice there, sometimes it's not. They're nice to you for a while, until the price has been paid, then they're just the same as the rest . . . the beatings start again.'

Suddenly stars appeared before my eyes and I felt my head slam into my friends head, I had to scream out at the pain . . . but not enough that I didn't hear the adult's voice.

'SO! . . . caught you, have I? What the hell do you think you're doing? The bell calling you in went ten minutes ago. You think this place runs on your rules, do you? Well, we'll soon teach you who runs this place.'

I was forced to my knees and then to my feet through the fact that whoever the adult was, he had a very strong grip of my hair.

The thin bamboo cane descended on my hands for what seemed an eternity . . . one . . . two . . . three . . . four . . . the pain became too much to bear and I pulled my hand back, the rest of the words and the beating where lost to my ears . . . I know I welcomed the blackness gratefully.

My friend was taken away a few weeks later by some adults and the last I saw of him was when I stood at one of the windows and waved goodbye to him. He didn't like to look at me, and hung his head down as he gave a small wave, then I watched him being forcibly dragged to a waiting car. I found myself disappointed that my friend hadn't fought harder. Long after the car had left, I was still on my knees at the window, looking sightlessly out at the world, and wondering what would happen to me if I was taken away. I vowed I would fight for my life every inch of the way through the gates, no adult would take me away that easily.

From here on in, my memory is a little vague as to what took place for a while. I can remember I seemed to be waking up in different beds for some time. There was also a kaleidoscope of smiling faces that seemed to fade and come back into view all the time. The voices also faded and rose according to the smiles on the faces.

Then on May 4, 1951, a hand was held out to me, and I reluctantly took it. Each step I took, took me nearer to the gates which had protected me from the horrors of the outside world.

I can remember turning around to look at the small faces pressed to the windows, each one solemn and lost in it's own thoughts, and for once I fought hard to go back to the only friends I had.

The horny skinned hand of Mr Faulk, my foster father, cracked against the side of my head with great force, lifting me bodily off my feet and slamming me down on the ground. The blow had been totally unexpected, and for a minute I wondered whether I had dreamt the whole thing. But the hot air of his voice in my ear told me I hadn't dreamt it up.

'The next time you laugh at Mrs Faulk, I'll beat you until you're black and blue. Just remember who you are, and the fact that without us, you wouldn't even have a home. Bastards have to be thankful for anything they receive.'

Mr Faulk was a tall, well built man, who worked at a tyre factory in Erdington, Brimingham. The work he did was heavily manual, which made his hands particularly painful when they came into contact with my head. He also liked to use his thick leather belt which was used to support his trousers along with the braces, when he wanted to give me a real beating. The belt was more than two inches wide, and was highly polished from much use. When he took it off and approached me with it hanging from his fist, I knew there was only one result. I would not be able to sit down for quite a few days, and my trousers would stick to the cuts as the blood dried.

Mrs Faulk was a woman who had a heart as cold as a brick. Most of her life she spent with her hair in curlers, and her false teeth gleaming at everybody from the magnified world of a water glass. And if she wasn't standing at the garden fence gossiping with a neighbour over a cup of tea, she was continually finding some reason to mistreat me, with the constant threat that she would tell Mr Faulk when he came home from work. She knew I feared the belt more than I feared a beating with the hand. When she wanted to beat me, she would take one of her slippers and beat me anywhere she could lay the slipper on my body.

Mrs Faulk was a woman whom I slowly began to realise took a secret delight in causing trouble for other people. And for some reason she got a great pleasure in watching me being beaten by her husband.

What was strange was the fact that I was not the only child in this household. The Faulks had their own child, a daughter some years older, called Jean who was adored by her parents and who could never ever do anything wrong.

Then there was another girl who was also fostered to the Faulk family like myself.

Her name was Sylvia Hackett, and she was no more than about two years older than myself. I was quick to learn she had a much more favoured position within the family than I could ever hope to attain. A fact she was not slow to use when she wanted to get me into trouble. But it took me a long time to realise that the only reason we were given a roof over our heads by the Faulk family was the fact they were being paid a considerable sum of money every month by the local council for looking after two foster children.

I started my life with the Faulk family in a house in Erdington. I realise now that my memories of this house were much better than those of the next house we moved to only six weeks after my arrival. The house we moved into was one of more than 200 terraced houses which were joined together in a long line stretching over half a mile. There was no garden, in contrast to the other house which even had a chicken shed. No, this house had been built in the 1920s, and the garden consisted of a long stretch of concrete bordered by a small amount of soil.

The house itself was tasteless and primitive, though there were enough rooms for each of us to have our own. I can even remember that for some years there was no bath in the house and it was necessary for me to stand naked in the kitchen in an old metal tub, whilst one of the girls poured water over me and Mrs Faulk scrubbed me brutally with carbolic soap and a floor scrubber. What was more embarrasing to me were the sniggers which came from Sylvia Hackett worsening my embarrasment of having to stand naked in front of her.

But the daughter of the house was rarely around, she had difficulty bringing herself to associate with us, especially me. I was a Bastard.

There were many things I was to experience at the hands of the Faulks, until the day I was finally taken away from them on the eighth of June, 1960. I was to experience things which only much later in my life did I realise were so brutal as to be almost inhuman. At this point I think it would be easier for me to give you an example of a typical day in the Faulk house.

Invariably Mr Faulk would rise at about six in the morning as he was required to start his work at seven o'clock. From my spartan bedroom I was sometimes able to watch him leave on his bicycle.

I should actually explain about this bedroom, it was both a dungeon and a place of sanctuary. The walls of the room were covered in a plain wallpaper which at times of rain showed stains from the water which had seeped through the brickwork.

The room itself was about ten feet long by about seven feet wide. In the right hand corner, on the outside wall was an old cast iron fireplace which they didn't find a necessity to block up or cover. Consequently, in the winter the snow fell down the chimney into the fireplace, the room temperature fell below freezing and the winds howled down the chimney rattling the heavy wooden door.

During the summer, when I was forced to go to bed at six o'clock in the evening, the room was filled with the sounds of children playing in the streets, and the sun streaming down the chimney into the room.

During the autumn, and times of rain, the fireplace would have a small pool of water under it. It was the time of year I hated most, because I received more and more brutal beatings, because Mrs Faulk was constantly accusing me of peeing into the fireplace. No amount of pleading on my behalf would change her mind, and I would have to wait in growing fear as the clock ticked around to the time Mr Faulk came home. Then the beatings with belt and slipper would start. Following that would come a week of nothing to drink to prevent me from peeing again into the fireplace. I lived in horror of waking up to find it had rained when a westerly wind had been blowing.

Next to the fireplace was a large window which looked out over the concrete garden, and then out onto a view of a very large church burial ground. I could see at least 600 marble crosses, some standing, some lying, some which had crashed over and fallen into the graves. Some nights I would stealthily creep from my bed and sit and watch the graveyard, waiting for the ghosts to leave their graves, always watching the shadows, some were real and some pretended. Then I would go back to bed, fear and sweat coating my skin as I thought about the next day.

Behind my bed and to the right of it was the heavy door. The door was nothing special, except for the fact that on the outside of it were two well oiled and heavy bolts. They were my nightmare . . . and my sanctuary. The nightmare was to be imprisoned in the room for thirteen-fourteen hours whilst other children were out playing; and the sanctuary was that I knew when I heard those bolts being pushed home at six o'clock in the evening, come rain wind or shine, I was fairly safe from another beating.

My room was totally devoid of any furniture except the bed. The floor was made up of plain wooden boards which had never been nailed down correctly or allowed to dry properly; consequently, when the room was very hot during the day, and then cooled at night, the floorboards would shrink and twist causing noises to reverberate throughout the house.

If the Faulks were sitting downstairs during the evening, then they would hear the noise and then I could be sure that within seconds one of them would be screaming at the door. When the noise failed to stop, Mr Faulk would be in my room, the belt swinging hard, because they believed I'd been out of bed moving around the room.

I was always the last one to be called from the room in the

morning. The daughter of the house usually got up first and had breakfast before I was allowed out of my room and an urgently needed toilet.

By the time I got downstairs to eat there was very little food left from the set amount Mr Faulk would allow to be put on the table. I would usually consider myself very lucky if I received a crust of buttered bread and a cold cup of tea for breakfast along with three slices of bread and meat drippings for lunch with the same for the evening meal. Every Sunday there would be meat on the table, which I would be allowed to have the remains of for a cold wash-day lunch on the Monday.

There was one thing I was allowed to eat in abundance, and that was potatoes; mashed, bashed, and boiled, in any quantity on the rare days they were served.

The eating habits of the Faulks were strange to say the least. I can say with all honesty, that if I was allowed to eat at the same table with them more than a dozen times in the nine years I lived there, then I was extremely lucky. Normally, I was sent outside to pace up and down in front of the kitchen window until the others had eaten, and then I was allowed inside to eat what was left, which was very little. For nine years, hunger was a constant companion. Asking for anymore food brought forth arguments on how I should think myself lucky I got anything to eat at all.

Because of the rationing going on at the time in England, I was required to attend the co-operative store where Mrs Faulk bought the food for the family. I was required to attend because she was still using the ration cards which were printed in my name for the issue of important basic foodstuffs which I was supposed to consume for a healthy growth. Needless to say, I never saw any of these important foodstuffs.

It was within a very short time of moving to the new house that a council welfare visitor came. The visits in themselves were supposed to be totally random so that the welfare people could check on the well-being of the children in care. But as I was soon to find out, the visits were planned well in advance so that even the Faulks knew exactly on which day the people would be coming.

On these days, I would invariably find myself suddenly locked into my room with the sternest of warnings to remain quiet, or, on the rare occasions I had to face the visitor, I was far too scared to voice the truth about the hell I was living in. I often wished the visitor would take me somewhere private where I could tell them of the horrors. But I also knew I was deluding myself, because if any one listened to what I said, they would challenge the Faulks who would deny it all, and then I would have to face the music after the people had left.

During these visits, Mrs Faulk always presented the visitor with a thick wad of bills for the clothes she had alledgedly bought for us, and then in return she would receive a fat cheque a few days later. I had often wondered if I could screw up the courage to tell the visitor that the clothes bought for the two foster children were bought from junk shops and flea markets. They were patched and worn out clothes and shoes which no one else could wear . . . except the foster children of the Faulks. But where did the receipts come from for the supposed new clothes? From members of her family who also had children, and from the neighbours. In her over the fence gossiping, she would wheedle the bills out of the people under one pretext or another, and then present them as her own. I can truly say there was only one thing I ever received new, and that was a pair of hob nailed boots from an Army and Navy surplus store. These boots were so special to me, that in my mind I turned them into magic boots which could walk me away from all the beatings and horrors.

In fact, my life as a child became an illusion. Whenever I returned to the house I would creep into my make believe world, to be able to shut out incessant complaints about myself which came from the toothless mouth of Mrs Faulk. I had become so good at disappearing into my own world, that I could look at her mouth moving and not hear a word she was saying. Instead, I was on the high seas as a pirate plundering a ship, or I was a fighter pilot shooting down the enemy, or I was an intrepid explorer discovering some land which I wasn't even sure existed.

From all these experiences in my illusionary world, I would write little stories on pieces of paper or old envelopes, and receive severe beatings because the Faulks assumed that I'd been reading books, something which for them was nothing but a waste of time and money. The nearest the Faulks house came to reading material was a copy of The Daily Mirror which was brought home from the tyre factory.

Each day that the rains fell, I would stand at the kitchen table and fill the old envelopes with stories from my illusionary world, and could be sure I would receive a beating . . . but I couldn't stop myself . . . the urge to write was too strong.

Between the tears and the constant pleadings to a silent God to help me, I lived and survived in this illusionary world.

Every day my boots carried me away from this horror to the school, but even there I was unable to escape the barbed tongues of the teachers and the children. I was often hauled out in front of the class to be made a public exhibition of. Dressed in my faded and patched grey shorts, grey socks, grey pulley and grey shirt, with my heavy hob nailed boots lacing half way up my leg, I was not a pretty sight. My hair was rarely combed and my magic boots were always dirty; boot polish in the Faulks house for someone like me, was considered too much of a luxury; a luxury that could be done without.

The whole class would laugh at the wartime refugee who was dressed in charity hand-outs, and the teachers did nothing to prevent it. After all, wasn't I a Bastard. Someone whose mother had had a child without getting married. There was only one type of woman who would do things like that, and it didn't take the inquisitive mind of a child long to come up with the answer.

Many was the night I lay in bed, unable to stop the endless tears, the interminable question never answered. Why? And why me? Is this what this world was all about? Why was it I could never laugh? Why was it I could only watch the other children playing outside, from the window of my prison room? God never helped me, no matter how much I pleaded; the beatings and cruelty still went on. Neither could he provide the answers to my questions.

So more and more I looked forward to the sanctuary of my room, where I would wait for the sound of the well oiled bolts sliding into place. Then my mind would release my soul to the world of illusion, then, and only then was I truly happy.

Up to now, and I was already eight years old, I had never actually been in a real fight, partly due to the fact that the

Faulks allowed me no contact with the other children outside of school time. But one day, I received a shock which stayed with me for a long time. I was a coward.

My first fight had developed from insults being thrown at me by other children, insults which went deep down inside me. The insults were about my mother . . . my real mother.

Even though I didn't even know of her existence, she had slowly developed in my mind until she seemed like a real person. She was soft and gentle, always smiling, ready to help. She was everything my dream world could conjure up about how I would like my real mother to be. So, it was inevitable that when the others began to call her names, I tried to defend her. The blows were swift and furious, and suddenly I realised I didn't know the first thing about fighting, all I could do was to curl up into a ball and wait for the blows to stop coming. That was something which I was very experienced in, I had learnt to take the blows but I hadn't learnt how to deliver them.

With deep shame I ran home and told the Faulks what had happened, and to my horror I received another beating with the belt that night when Mr Faulk returned home. Not because I'd been fighting, but because I'd lost the fight and run away. I had brought further shame on them.

'Not only are you a Bastard. But you're a cowardly Bastard; and that's even worse!'

The words were punctuated with beatings from the belt until I cowered on the floor my arms over my head, legs drawn up into a foetal position.

It was inevitable I would become the butt end of everyone else's bad jokes in the school, the school bullies had a field day kicking the coward as he ran home from school. Even my so called step sister, Sylvia Hackett, wanted nothing further to do with me. She walked home from school with her friends, never once recognising me on the road. Finally I learnt to walk alone, and to keep a wary eye on my back; watching for any of the schoolboys who loved to sneak up on me and spit on the coward of a refugee.

I suppose it was inevitable I would finally get into trouble. For a little while I had been helping myself to food from the school kitchens, to ease the ravenous hunger which lurked inside of me. I knew it was no point in asking for more food at home, because I wouldn't get it. But the food I was helping myself to in the school kitchens was for the other children's school lunches. I was stealing food to survive . . . and I got caught.

All hell broke loose then. The Faulks were called to the school by the headmaster and given a severe talking to about their foster son. There's no further need for me to tell you what happened after that. Somehow or other I was allowed to stay at the school, but the emotional cost to myself was enormous. Now the jokes became cruel, and the beatings more and more frequent. Slowly I began to fight back more and more until one day something happened.

The hunger inside me had become more and more uncontrollable as I grew. Sometimes I would lie awake at night with pains in my stomach. I was thin already, and getting thinner all the time.

I was stealing food from shops to be able to eat. I stole bread from the delivery vans that called around the houses. I spent almost all of my waking hours trying to find something to eat, and still I got thinner. The skin barely covered my ribs as I stole bottles of milk from the doorsteps early in the mornings on my way to school. It couldn't go on . . . and it didn't. This time the police were called and I was taken to the police station.

For once in my short life, I was alone with someone in a room who really wanted to know why I had been stealing food all this time. And I told him, and told him, and told him. I left nothing out. When the Faulks came to the police station to collect me, they were taken into a separate room and questioned for some time.

When I got home that night nothing was said to me, and the customary beating never occurred. The Faulks never said a word, and that really frightened me.

For more than two weeks I never received a single beating. But the looks I got over a silent and empty table more than made up for it. By the time I went to bed I was a bag of nerves from the psychological torture. I could no longer slip into my dream world, all I could do was to lie in bed, my bedclothes sticking to my sweating body as I waited for the explosion to come. I lost more weight, my clothes hung from me like rags. At school I was getting more and more trouble with the boys who beat and jostled me with impunity. I would often run home with my pullover full of the spit which had been rained down on me. And I stole even more food, chocolate, sweets, anything I could get my hands on.

Yes. It came to a sudden end when I was caught in a shop stealing a handful of broken biscuits from a jar. The value of what I'd stolen came to one penny, but for that one penny an episode in my life came to an end. The police were called again, and this time I was unceremoniously hauled off to the police station by a good old English bobby who had a very good grip on my ear.

'I'm sorry Mr Faulk. I understand how you feel, but we are not allowed to put children under twelve years of age into prison cells. Only a magistrate can do that. Secondly, Mr Faulk, there are some disturbing facts about this boy which we feel will have to be investigated further.'

The big beefy red-faced police sergeant stood in front of Mr Faulk, rocking gently backwards and forward on his heels. He was almost daring Mr Faulk to say something, but there was only silence.

'Why don't you take him home Mr Faulk and somebody will be around to see you in the next day or so.'

I followed my foster father out of the police station and stood on the pavement as he turned to look at me.

'You're finished. Do you know that? You're finished! We don't want you any more. Never have I come across someone who is so ungrateful for the kind help that he's been given. Is this how you pay us back for all we've done for you? You have your own room in the house, you get three meals a day and everything you want. Then you have to go stealing. If you're so hungry why didn't you tell us?'

I could only look down at the pavement, there was no point in telling him my side of the story. Suddenly I felt his iron grip on my shoulder and waited for the blows, but he must have remembered where he was and his hand slid off my shoulder.

By the time I got up the following morning I realised I hadn't heard the bolts being drawn on my door. Something so unusual as that drew my eyes to the door as I left the room, the bolts were missing and the holes had been painted over. It was as if they had never been there.

Trouble started for me before I even got to the school. All

the boys who saw me, seemed to know what had happened the day before. They hurled every kind of abuse at me, and all I did was to keep walking, my head bowed to the ground. It was during the school break the real trouble started.

The school bully, a boy called John Davies, saw me trying to hide myself in a corner of the playground. He approached me in his nonchalant macho style with half a dozen of his cronies to back him up. Each one was giving moral support to the other, the entire group giving support to everyone.

Sitting there on the floor, watching the group approaching, their intrepid leader chewing his gum like some camel grinding his teeth, suddenly brought a clarity to my head that was like the bursting of a distant star. The light shone in my mind and suddenly I knew where I really stood. Was it not true that society had long ago declared war on me? Not for something that I'd done, no! But for something my mother had done! Was it not true that society had not once listened to my pleas for help? Was it not true that those who should be helping me had turned away from me? Was it not true that as far as society was concerned, I was just a burden, an embarrassment, a headache? Was it not true that I had been spat on so many times that my entire skin burnt with the humiliation? Was it not true that I'd been kicked and beaten so often my body was almost immune to any more pain? Was it not true that I was already in more than enough trouble? Was it not true that the world would breathe a sigh of relief without me? Then so be it. But before I went, I would show the world why I carried so many scars.

I took a few deep breaths and felt an immenseness of spirit which my puny frame seemed hardly big enough to hold. I didn't jump up quickly or anything. I just casually got up and faced the group of boys, because suddenly that was all they were, boys on an ego trip. The constant gyrations of Davis's mouth only stopped when he talked, I could imagine him standing in front of a mirror practising his Elvis Presley stance. I saw him with a clarity of vision that was unbelievable.

'Heh you. Where's your mother then? Gone back on the streets to earn some more money?'

The whole group laughed when he laughed, and stopped when he stopped. Nothing more than puppets. All I did was to smile up at him, he was at least a head taller and thirty pounds heavier.

'I hear tell you're a thief Dawson, been stealing. We don't like thieves, Dawson. Do you know what we do to thieves . . . Dawson? We teach 'em a lesson . . . one they won't forget in a very long time. Do you know what we do to Bastards who are thieves? . . . We teach them an even bigger lesson . . . we hurt them. Do you know what we're going to do to you? . . . We're gonna' hurt you.'

I saw him glance over his shoulder ostensibly to check there were no teachers about, but he was checking to see that all his friends were with him. He signalled for two of the boys to pin me against the wall, and I allowed them to do so. Davis was my target.

Inside me was a calm which I would never have believed possible. Then suddenly one of his friends cried out.

'Here . . . just a minute. I recognise that pullover he's got on.'

The boy moved forward and pulled the garment over my head. True enough, there was his name tag sewn on a seam inside the arm. Suddenly he was jubilant.

'Heh . . . he's stolen one of my pulleys . . . would you believe it? . . . how did he get his thieving hands on this?'

He swung around to hit me, but Davis stopped him, a smile on his face.

'That's my job mate . . . or do you want to take over?'

The boy blanched and backed away, a coward all the way to the soles of his shoes. I didn't bother to tell Davis that the pulley had been bought by my foster mother in the rag market in Erdington. What was the point? I would just be wasting my breath.

Davis advanced on me, making a fist of his right hand and waving it about to enable him to build up his courage . . . oh yes, the picture was absolutely clear. And then he was within range.

I will always be grateful to the Faulks for buying me those hob nailed boots from the Army and Navy store. They were heavy and made to withstand a lot of punishment. And when my foot came up between Davis's legs, there was all the power I could put behind the blow. Suddenly a bright red ball of fire burst inside my head and filled me with an unbelievable feeling of power, my course was decided, and the risk accepted.

I fought as someone who had never had anything to lose, and took Davis apart. Screams filled the air, blood flowed freely, and suddenly I was in part repaying the world for the cruelty I had suffered on it's behalf.

When the burning light in my head had burnt out, I found myself standing over Davis who was lying face down on the ground whimpering. His friends had long ago deserted him and a hushed silence was over the playground. I turned to face the multitude and with my fists still balled and covered in blood I walked out of the school never to return. I was then twelve and a half years old and had stepped over some unknown border. I knew that from now on, there would be no going back.

★   ★   ★   ★

They found me down by the river which meandered lazily through the trees. Without really realising it, I had fallen asleep whilst watching the dancing sunlight on the water's surface. It had been an untroubled and for the first time, a very peaceful sleep.

When I turned around and saw the big black boots under the blue uniform there was no need for me to look who it was.

'Come on, young man. There's no point in running any more, it's not going to help you.'

Oh, how wrong he was. I hadn't been running from anything or anyone. I'd just chosen the where and the when that they would arrest me, as I surely knew they would do.

I got up off the warm ground and stood facing the red faced sergeant.

'How did you know where to find me?'

The man smiled as he put his hand on my shoulder and walked me back to the road.

'Many hundreds of years ago, I was in a similar situation as you, not like with your foster parents, but with a school bully. I also had to get away somewhere quiet. Here there are but two possibilities to be quiet. In the churchyard sitting on some gravestone, or here by the river. That's where I would look for someone like you.'

The talks went on for many hours, first there had been lots

of questions about what I'd been stealing and why. And then there were more questions about the fight with Davis. It seemed as though I was in serious trouble.

But then the questions stopped, and I was finally being listened to. So I talked and talked and the grim faced men listened and listened.

When they asked me if I was hungry, I told them how hungry I was. And when the meal arrived, a steaming plate of bacon and eggs, sausage and tomato, I could only believe I was in fact sitting in heaven. Such wonderful fare I'd rarely seen in my twelve years of life.

It was when I'd finished the meal that the florid faced station sergeant came into the room and sat down opposite me. Just the questioning look on his face told me I was in trouble.

'What are you going to do now, young Dawson?'

I could feel my eyebrows knitting together as I tried to work out what he was talking about. Something must have softened the man's heart because he decided not to prolong the agony.

'I've just spoken to your foster parents. They have refused to have you back home. They are of the impression you are a liar and thief of the first grade. They say your stories about being starved are absolute lies, and they've never ever locked you in the bedroom. They say you've always been free to come and go as you want, and that you were only kept at home as a punishment when you were naughty.'

I felt as though the wind had been kicked forcibly out of my body. The way the sergeant had related everything, gave me the distinct impression that no one was prepared to believe anything I said. That two people could lie so much, and be believed by the people who were invested with the authority to protect all, seemed unbelievable. It seemed the state could never be wrong, even in the choice of my foster parents.

'The welfare people have already tried to persuade your foster parents to reconsider their decision. They are adamant; they do not want you back.'

I asked the question which nearly choked me to get out.

'What is going to happen to me now?'

The fat policeman looked at me for sometime, as if he was working out just how honest he could be. Finally he'd made his mind up in my favour.

'We're going to have to keep you here for a few days until

the weekend is over.'

Suddenly my heart seemed to lift to the heavens.

'Does that mean I shall never have to go back to . . . the foster parents?'

His eyes narrowed as he felt my excitement.

'Yes . . . but don't think it will be nice here. We are going to have to put you into a holding cell as there's no one here to look after you. You'll be in there for at least twenty-three hours a day as we can't treat you any different to other prisoners.'

I had no experience of what he was trying to tell me, but whatever it was, it couldn't be worse than what I'd already been through.

'What will happen to me after that?'

I knew whatever he was going to say, he didn't like it. It visibly took some effort for him to get it out.

'I think you deserve to be told the truth. Your foster parents don't want you, and you're too old to be adopted or fostered out to other parents. And the local council does not have homes for boys of your age. It's almost certain you will have to appear before the magistrates, who will, make their decision as to your future . . . I think you'll end up in an approved school . . . it's a fancy word for a young offenders' prison . . . you'll be there for the minimum time of three years.'

I could not feel my body as I followed the sergeant down into the bowels of the police station. I was in shock . . . deep shock. I would be going to prison for three years . . . for being hungry and needing food. It seemed clear to me that someone preferred me to be dead. What else could I do when I was starving hungry? I'd learnt that words don't fill an empty stomach, and asking for more food only got me severe beatings.

My head spun as I descended the concrete steps, frustration welled up inside of me, I couldn't understand why I had been given a mouth to talk, if that which I said was never heard. I felt as though I was screaming into a hot desert, and the grains of sand represented the people. The more I screamed for help the more the hot air carried my words away from the ears of the people. Was hunger a crime? . . . a crime so bad that I should be put into a . . . prison . . . for a minimum of three years? . . . It would seem so.

The heavy steel door shut behind me and I could hear the key being turned in the lock. I slumped down on the ground with my back against the massive structure of the door and looked around me. I could feel the impregnable density of the walls around me, where even the forces of life could no longer penetrate.

I looked across to the iron cot which was bolted and concreted into the floor, the single grey hairy blanket folded neatly on the rubber sheeted mattress. I looked, too, at the single bucket which stood in the corner of the cell. There was no need to ask what that was for.

I looked at the grey and cream walls which bore the last messages of previous occupants, the messages of undying love, names written to evoke memories of . . . of . . . another world. My eyes strayed to the heavy thick glass frame set high in the wall. It was designed to allow only the rays of light into the cell, the glass being so thick I couldn't even see the sky through it; and I listened . . . I listened to the immense silence . . . the total silence . . . and felt my heart fall to the deepest depths of hell. The shock was so much I couldn't even cry, I couldn't even feel the presence of my heart anymore. The only thing I could do . . . was to scream . . . a long, wailing, heart racking scream. It didn't matter anymore, there was no one to hear me, I was buried beneath the ground.

The court room, was an immense oak panelled room, with large ornate wooden chairs for the judges, ornate benches for the lawyers, benches for the public . . . and for me, a plain wooden box to stand up in with a stout policeman blocking the only way out of it. I could feel the immensity of power in this room, but as I looked at the magistrate who was bent over his papers, I wondered how many illegitimate children he'd brought into the world.

It was not hard for me to realise that here my future was to be decided according to the content of the magistrates stomach. If it sat well with him, then the man would be lenient, but if he'd got problems with his family, then I would be the whipping boy for all that was wrong. Yes . . . I'd gone into a prison cell a twelve-year-old boy . . . stayed in that hell for more than seventy-two hours ... alone ... with only the walls to hear my pleas. But when I had come out ... it had been as a wiser man, the state had declared war against me, so be it ... they understood only one thing.

I looked across to the court orderly who was reading my name and details out to the court. His voice droned on like some fly against the glass, soon it faded from my mind as I found myself asking questions.

Had my twelve years on this earth really been so bad? What about the two years I'd been a choir boy in the Erdington Parish Church. Hadn't that been fun? Looking at Girlie magazines hidden behind our hymn books, the church-goers smiling at the twenty-four saintly cassocked and ruffled choir-boys as they walked down through the church to the altar, whilst the choir master Mr MacCallister with the hare lip, hammered away at the organ. Weddings, funerals, Sunday services, midnight mass at Christmas, christenings and any other religious things that could be dreamt up.

We, the choir boys, had sung dirty songs to traditional tunes whilst the ignorant church-goers had listened enraptured to our heavenly voices and not understood a single word. And we'd been paid handsomely for our indiscretions. But alas, that was were the fun had ended. All monies I'd earnt in the church had to be given to the foster parents to help pay back some of that which they had so generously spent on me.

What about the paper round? Hadn't that been fun? Delivering *The Times* newspaper to Mr Thomas who was a refuse collector and giving Mr Green the company director, a copy of the *Daily Mirror*. A copy of *Woman's Weekly* to young Mr Lassiter and a copy of the latest sex magazine to old Mrs Roland, a devout church goer and spinster of this parish. Oh yes, I'd lit some fires under a few backsides, and had a belt across my own as well. The proceeds of this work also disappeared into the pockets of the Faulks.

What about Christmas time? That was great fun opening a Christmas present wrapped in brown paper, only to have fall out a worn out second hand torch which had been bought in the flea market. No one had bothered to buy batteries for it, and it was doubtful if the bulb had ever worked. Great fun, smashing Christmas. If that was all the world had to offer me, then whatever this bad tempered magistrate was going to do, it couldn't get any worse.

'Do you agree with all the details . . . Dawson?'

I looked a little startled across to the magistrate, after the policeman's elbow had almost broken two of my ribs, I thought I wouldn't be able to get my breath to answer the man.

'Err . . . yes.'

I had absoultely no idea what had been said, and nobody was prepared to go over it again.

'I want you to listen to what the Clerk of the Court has to say, and then tell me if you agree with it?'

I nodded my head at the magistrate and turned to watch the Clerk of the Court. The man lifted a stack of papers and cleared his throat . . . had I done so much that it needed so much paper?

'On the First of June this year . . . Dawson was arrested for stealing exactly one handful of broken biscuits from a jar in Liptons shop on the High Street, Erdington. The arrest took place at the insistence of the shop manager, even though technically the accused is under age.'

The unblinking gaze of the magistrate turned in my direction, he was used to dealing with hardened criminals and knew how to intimidate them with his gaze. And believe me, when I say that I was so frightened I could have filled my trousers.

'What do you have to say to this charge Dawson . . .?'

The discreet clearing of the Clerk's throat brought the magistrate to attention.

'There are a further six charges of theft against Dawson, all of them involving the stealing of food. They are listed on the charge sheet in front of you. Do you wish me to read them out?'

Again the cold eyes turned to me.

'Do you have anything to say, Dawson?'

I could only shake my head.

'No need to read the rest out. Bring in the arresting officer.'

The red faced Sergeant strode into the court and stood in the witness box. He took the oath to tell the truth and then opened his pocket book.

'I arrested Dawson at Liptons, after the manager of the shop had strenuously insisted I do so. The accused was found with a handful of broken biscuits which he was unable to pay for. I cautioned the accused and took him to the Police Station.'

'Why did he steal the biscuits?'

The policeman slowly closed the book and put it into his breast pocket.

'Hunger . . . the accused was hungry.'

Sarcasm whipped through the court like a tornado.

'That doesn't give the accused the right to steal. If everybody went stealing when they were hungry . . . we'd be in a right mess. What do the parents of this . . . the accused have to say?'

A man who up to now had been sitting in the public benches got up and asked permission to come forward. It was grudgingly granted.

'My name is Walters, and I'm from the local children's department. The boy Dawson is here under the care of foster parents . . . unfortunately the foster parents have relinquished their guardianship over the child since this . . . incident.'

'What does that mean?'

'It means, your Honour, that the boy Dawson has been returned to the care of the local council.'

'Where are the foster parents?'

I saw the Faulks get up from their seats somewhere at the back of the court. He walked hat in hand like some beggar, whilst she held onto his coat following him. They shuffled their way to the front of the court in an abject manner, the act of a simple couple was almost convincing, even to me. This was a totally different people to the ones I'd lived with. Where were the bared teeth as he beat me? And where were the balled fists that had clubbed me across the head as she screamed me down until I was cowering on the floor? Butter could not have melted in the mouths of the two people facing the court.

'You've heard the charge against this . . . the accused. What do you have to say?'

Mr Faulk turned his hat through his hands, his knees slightly bent as he looked up to the almighty magistrate.

'Your Lordship . . .'

'It's enough when you say, Your Honour'.

The Clerk of the Court said it in such a way as to make me realise he wasn't so taken in as the rest of the court.

'Yes, Your Lordship . . . I . . . err . . . we . . . that is . . .

my wife and I have given this . . . Geoffrey a home for the last nine years. We did it even though we knew about his . . . from where he came . . .'

The Clerk of the Court rose and whispered something to the Magistrate, who's malevolent eye swung around to me . . . Now he knew he had a Bastard in the court . . . in his court.

'We gave him all that we could from our meager money to make him happy, we accepted him with the goodness of our hearts. Even our only child welcomed him as a brother . . . an . . . equal brother. How he has repaid us for our kindness . . . has broken my wife's heart.'

There was the slightest sound of someone blowing into a handkerchief behind his back, I didn't need to ask who it was.

'Is it true, you don't want him back in your home?' Faulk bowed his head.

'I'm sorry your Lordship . . . your honour . . . but for my wife and daughter and the other foster child . . . having the police at our home is getting too much . . . we're not so young to be able to stand the worry.'

The magistrate sat quietly looking down at his notes, finally he looked down at the Faulks.

'Is that your last word?'

The two of them bowed their heads.

'You can leave. Who is here for the prosecution?'

A young man stood up, his black robe catching in the chair.

'Anything you have to say?'

'Yes, your Honour. Umm . . . as the accused is under age for criminal charges, what we have here is not really admissable. But I would like to make the court aware of a few facts. When the accused was brought into the police station and questioned, he made some very wild charges against his foster parents. Charges which we were forced to establish the truth of. He said that they beat him continuously and that he was kept prisoner in a locked and bare room overnight, and that he rarely got enough to eat, being given only what was left over from the parents' meal. Upon an unannounced arrival at the foster parents' home, we asked to have a look at the accused's room. It was found to be light, well aired, with lots of sweets which were kept in a very large bottle . . .'

I knew where all that had come from, from their own daughter's room. It was all lies and I was the one telling them.

You can't fight the state, and the state had picked my foster parents . . . the state was never wrong.

'As to the claim that the room was bolted from outside. We found that the door and frame had been freshly painted, but Mr Faulk says that was done a short while ago because the door was made so dirty . . . by the accused. Since the accused has been in custody he has been examined by a police doctor who has declared that the accused is seriously underweight, but thinks it could just be due to his fast rate of growth. In any event, the kitchen where the accused lived, was inspected and found to be adequately stocked considering the size of the family and the money available. It is our opinion that the accused stole for the sake of stealing, and without any need for what he stole.'

I felt as if the breath had been steamrollered out of me. How anybody could stand before the court and tell such lies, was now beyond me. I realised there was no such thing as the truth, only the degree to which the lies were beliveable. I could feel my soul falling to the floor as the world again turned against me. What had I done to them? Was being born, the sin I had committed? If being dead would satisfy them, then they could happily take my life.

'Who is here for the accused?'

All eyes looked around the court, but no one came forward . . . except the man from the children's office.

'Umm . . . as Dawson is under age . . . there's no legal aid granted . . . so we thought it unnecessary to provide a lawyer . . . there are no real charges against him. It is just necessary for the court to make a decision as to . . . err. . . Dawson's future.'

'And what does the Children's Department want?'

The man walked forward and laid his briefcase on a desk, then faced the magistrate. His calmness told me a decision had been long ago made. He was about to pronounce the death sentence on me. Suddenly I felt so calm. Was such a sentence so easily reached.

'Your Honour. Having taken all the facts into consideration, and heard the Faulk's side, it is the opinion of the Children's Department that Dawson requires a very close supervision. We, the Children's Department are not equipped to provide the sort of supervision Dawson needs. We also think it would be better if he was placed into a closed institution. Better for himself, and better for the public.

After consideration, we would like to ask the court to rescind the parental right order given to the Children's Department; and to place Dawson in an approved school at least until he is fifteen and a half years old.'

I could no longer hear anything. There was a rushing sound in my ears, my heart was hammering at the walls of my chest. Three years . . . three years in prison . . . for being hungry. I had stolen to survive . . . and that was the penalty . . . for being an embarrassment to the state. I looked at the faces, but only saw the mouths moving, no words came to my ears.

The magistrate leaned over the bench and spoke in whispers to the Clerk of the Court, then the two men nodded their heads.

'Dawson. It is the decision of this court, in the light of everything we've heard, to grant the Children's Department its wish and to place you in a closed institution for at least three years. Have you anything further to say?'

He most probably thought my silence was insolence, but I truly had not heard one word, my head was buzzing. Which was most probably why he smashed the gavel down on the block.

'Case closed. Prisoner is dismissed.'

I looked again at the walls of my cell, seeing them as someone who would be spending a great deal of time there. Their solidity was reassuring, but the silence within the cell was nerve destroying. To all intent and purpose, the real world didn't exist outside of this cell. It was a different cell to where I had spent the last few days. I was in the holding cells underneath the court rooms, and these cells had seen a lot of people passing through them. The walls were dirty and bore the signatures of many a prisoner and underneath the sentence they had received.

How they had managed to scratch their name onto the brickwork was beyound my understanding because when I was put into my cell, I was stripped of shoes, belt, tie, and anything which could be used by the wildest imagination to either escape or to commit suicide. They had even gone to the extent of forcing my mouth open to see if I had false teeth.

I studied the signatures at length, time was of no

consequence. There were people who had been sentenced from six months to twenty-five years. One could only guess what they'd been doing.

From within the bowels of the building I suddenly heard the sound of someone whistling. Like a drowning man I ran to the door and placed my ear against the cold thick metal. There it was again, slowly approaching, another human being; I was not alone.

Where the sound was coming from I did not know, but it seemed to take an eternity to wind it's way through the maze of corridors. Then suddenly I realised that whoever it was, they were coming for me. I ran back from the door and placed my back against the far wall, as I'd been instructed to do by the sergeant in Erdington. Suddenly a small flap was opened in the door and a pair of eyes studied me.

'Stay where you are.'

The flap closed and there was the rattling of keys, then the door swung open and in walked a policeman carrying a large tray.

'The Sergeant from Erdington has bought and paid for a lunch he says you'll like. It's fish and chips and a pint of milk. Here, sit on the bed and enjoy the meal. It's the last you'll get here as you'll be on the first part of your long journey to the approved school this afternoon.'

The policeman withdrew and left me alone to marvel at the plate of food on the tray. I'd only seen such a good meal twice in my life, and that was only whilst I'd been in prison. I devoured the food with relish, finishing it off with the milk. I was feeling quite good when suddenly the door of the cell crashed open with force, slamming back against the wall. I was so shocked at the suddenness of the move that I jumped to my feet, the tray crashing to the floor, the last of the milk staining my trousers. Standing in front of me was a big policeman, legs spread, arms on hips . . . he was wide and mean.

'Ok, you. Get your shoes on and be quick about it. Move!'

I looked around, confused. I didn't know where my shoes where. And I was trying to pick up the tray and contents. There was no way of knowing what I should do first. Then I saw his left hand pointing down to the floor outside the cell. He was showing me where my shoes were.

With my back to the wall, and a wary eye on the big man I quickly put my shoes on. Then I stood up.

'Did you eat what was on that plate?'

'Err . . . yes.

'Then you've got the strength to carry it. What do you think this place is . . . a hotel? My God lad, we shall have to get you straightened out, and where you're going is just the place for you.'

The way it was said, made me wonder just what was in store for me. Such was the effect his words had on me, I did not dare to ask if I could use the toilet. Instead I picked up my tray and followed the gruff man out into the corridor, and then followed his back down the long passages. As we approached the door leading out into the world of the living, a voice broke the silence.

'You cradle snatching now, copper?'

I looked around me for the source of the voice, but all there was to see, were the lines of locked steel doors on both sides of me. The policeman snarled at whoever the voice belonged to.

'Shut your mouth Mulligan, or I'm liable to come in there and shut if for you.'

Then his booted foot flashed out and kicked one of the steel doors a mighty blow. There was a cackling laughter from the other side of the door.

'Watch him, kid. He's a mean bastard that copper is. He loves hitting people, especially those smaller than himself.'

The voice was suddenly cut off as the big man pulled me by the scruff of the neck through another door and slammed it to.

'Tray.'

I looked to where the finger pointed and then put the tray down on the shelf.

'Left or right handed?'

I know I must have looked at the man a little stupidly, but how was I to know what he was talking about. His eyes turned cold on me.

'Are you right handed, or are you left handed. What does it take to get through your thick skull?'

'Right handed.'

'Stick it out.'

When someone told me to stick my hand out, it usually meant I was about to be beaten, it was only natural I was cautious.

'I said stick it out!'

His hand descended on my shoulder and squeezed unmercifully. I stuck my hand out, only to stop the pain. Immediately a cold band of steel encircled my wrist and snapped to with a disturbing finality. Then he took a key from his trouser pocket and opened a door which fitted so well into the wall I'd not even noticed it.

I was forced to shield my eyes against the brilliant sunshine as I was almost dragged by my outstretched arm towards a dark blue van sitting in the middle of the yard. Standing next to the van was another policeman who opened the doors of the vehicle as I approached. Sitting inside the vehicle, on hard wooden slat benches were eight other 'prisoners' whose hands were handcuffed to the benches.

I had to scramble to keep my feet, as a heavy hand pushed me into the back of the vehicle and quickly attached me to the woodwork. Then the doors were closed and darkness descended until my eyes were able to adjust to the dim light. I looked at the young man who sat next to me, the grin on his face said he was enjoying himself.

'This your first time?'

'First time?'

He nodded his head.

'It's your first time. What did you do. Kill someone? You're a bit young to be handcuffed and shipped off to the cells.'

'I . . . I . . . stole some food.'

The laugh was rough and brutal.

'Oh come one. Don't give me such shit. You don't get the top security treatment for stealing food. All right . . . if you don't want to tell me . . . then don't. But the truth will come out when you're in the remand home.'

The van rocked and lurched it's way out onto the road and began its journey. I strained my neck to look out of the darkened windows and felt a hole growing inside me. That was my world out there, for good or for bad, that was my world. People walking in the sun, buildings bathed in sun, birds and animals moving around . . . free . . . in freedom. I could be forgiven for wondering if I would ever see the sun again as I sat in this darkened prison van.

'How long did they give you then?

'Who?'

'Jesus . . . you really are green. The Beak . . . the Magistrate, how long did he bang you down for . . . how long did he put you away for? Six months . . . three months . . . nine months . . .?'

Suddenly I understood what he meant.

'Three years.'

He looked at me with surprise.

'You must be a hard one then. Three years is the maximum. It's the equivalent sentence for an adult who's committed murder. How old are you?'

'Twelve.'

By now the rest of the occupants were following the conversations. There were whispered words of amazement.

'Jesus . . . you must have upset someone. Did you really only steal food? You didn't clobber anyone for it . . . like . . . you didn't get done for GBH . . . you know grevious bodily harm . . . or something?'

I thought about the court case and couldn't remember anyone saying anything about . . . GBH.

'I was in a fight with a school bully before I was arrested . . . but . . . no . . . I only stole some food . . . I was so hungry.'

My companion shook his head in disbelief.

'Where did you get knocked down . . . who was the Beak?'

He saw my lack of understanding and tried again.

'Which court did you get tried at, and who was the Magistrate?

'It was here, where we've just come from. I don't know who the Magistrate was. He was bad tempered, wore glasses, bald headed.'

My companion sucked in his breath sharply.

'That was Holman . . . nick named the Vulture. Come up before him and you're lucky if you leave his court alive and breathing. They usually only send the real hard cases to him . . . you know . . . GBH . . . Armed Robbery . . . Murder . . . Manslaughter . . .'

'But I thought he was only a Magistrate . . . don't those sort of people go to . . . jails?'

Suddenly he laughed and slapped his knee with a free hand.

'You really are green. You must be the unluckiest sod that

ever walked this earth. Where we're going you'll meet kids
from fourteen years of age up to seventeen . . . eighteen . . .
even nineteen years old who've committed every crime written
into the statute books . . . Murder . . . Brutality . . . GBH . . .
Armed Robbery . . . Rape . . . sexual assault . . . buggery . . .
you name it, and I guarantee we'll find someone in there
who's done it.'

I sat back as far as my handcuff would allow and looked out
of the back window. As I watched the movement of the
people, I felt as though I no longer belonged to them. I was
going to another world, a world far away from where I'd been.
Had I been stupid? Why hadn't I just kept my mouth shut?
What was a daily beating and starvation, against what I was
going to now? A life among murderers . . . rapists . . . crooks
thieves . . . robbers . . . what was I going to?

2

The journey to wherever we were going seemed to take a long time . . . a fact I was glad for, because it delayed just a little longer the beginning of the end for me.

Then, almost before I could turn my head, we'd barrelled in through a set of high wrought iron gates which were shut behind us. My companion seemed to be well acquainted with this place the van was pulling up in front of.

'Well, mates. Here we are. Mosely Road remand home. The blokes who run this place are the ones the Germans didn't shoot, because they thought it was their own people in disguise.'

The van doors slammed back against the sides and let in the punishing sunlight. One of the police officers climbed into the vehicle and unfastened the handcuffs pushing us out one by one. There was more shouting and directions from two men who'd come from the building.

'All right, you lot. We don't have all day to stand around talking. Get inside . . . M-O-V-E.'

The commands were backed up with the switch of a bamboo cane in the hand of a very mean looking gentleman. I noticed very quickly that the two men carried a large and heavy bunch of keys on their belts. We all quickly crossed the free ground between the van and the front door under the careful scrutiny of the 'screws' who were just waiting for one of us to try and make a break for it. The front door closed solidly behind us, and I heard for the very first time the sound of a door being locked behind me; a sound that would become so familiar and to happen at least a million times that I wouldn't hear it anymore, only when it actually stopped did I suddenly realise it. The malevolent eyes of the screw fell on my companion from the vehicle.

'So Harris. You couldn't stand being away from us, eh. Missed our company did you? What did you do this time?'

He seemed a little reluctant to answer the question. The bamboo cane was shoved under his chin until his head was forced back against the door.

'I asked you a question.'

'GBH . . . sir.'

His head straightened up as the cane was slowly lowered, there was a smile on the screw's face.

'So. We didn't knock some brains into you the last time you were here. This time we'll make sure we don't make any mistakes. How long did you get?'

'Three years. sir.'

There was the slightest of hesitation when he said 'Sir'. There was a sudden movement from the screw and Harris was down on his knees, hands over his testicles, face turning almost green.

'Welcome to Mosely Road remand home, Harris. I can assure you we are most pleased to see you.'

I could feel the suppressed fears from the rest of the van's occupants, and was somewhat apprehensive myself. This was brutality on a different scale to what I'd experienced before. This was cold blooded, without emotion.

'Anybody else who's been here before?'

There was a general shaking of the heads.

'Call out your names, ages, charges, and sentences.'

He turned and took a clipboard from a man standing behind him, then turned slowly back to face us. His right hand reached up and stroked the luxurious moustache, then he suddenly pointed at me.

'You. Start.'

'Dawson . . . err . . . twelve years old . . . stealing food . . .'

'Start again! Dawson . . . twelve years old . . . robbery . . .'

I took a deep breath, trying to calm my nerves.

'Dawson . . . twelve years old . . . steal . . . robbery . . . three years.'

The bamboo cane suddenly lifted and slowly stabbed my chest until my back was against the wall.

'Do you stutter . . . boy?'

'No.'

The cane came down swiftly on the soft part of my shoulder near the neck, I could feel my knees giving way but forced myself to accept the pain without showing how much it had hurt.

'No . . . what.'

I fought back the tears and thought fast and furious, suddenly the answer was there.

'No, sir.'

The tight pinched face slowly smiled.

'See how easily you learn here. Faster than anywhere else in the whole land. I'm sure you'll never forget that lesson. If your parents had been so conscientious and loving to you . . . you wouldn't be here now.'

'I don't have any parents.'

The eyes suddenly narrowed, the expression on the face set hard, and the cane descended with a swoosh on the back of my hand. The shock of the blow nearly made me feel sick, and I was forced to take many a deep breath. I was forced back against the wall again.

'You seem to have forgotten your first lesson . . . boy.'

I could no longer see the man clearly, I was desperately trying to hold back the tears.

'Yes, sir.'

Suddenly the cane was taken away.

'Next one.'

The voices were nervous.

'Williams. Fourteen. Breaking and entering. Eighteen months, sir.'

'Brown. Fifteen. Arson. Eighteen months, sir.'

Lampert. Fourteen. Shop lifting. Six months, sir.'

'Smith. Fifteen. Shop lifting. Twelve months, sir.'

'Jansenn. Fifteen. Awaiting Her Majesty's Pleasure.'

You could have heard a pin drop. The silence was enormous. It was to be much later that I would find out just what the implication of such a sentence meant for the convicted and the screw.

The sentence 'Awaiting Her Majesty's Pleasure' meant only one thing. Murder of a gruesome nature, or a very serious crime committed with the loss of life. The convicted could be kept in a prison for the rest of his life, with nothing further to lose, regardless of what he did to anyone else, only being released when the authorities thought it safe to let him back into society. Whoever received such a sentence, was feared by the screws and was handled with a very short and brutal rein. A screw's life to a man so convicted meant less than that of a fly.

Each eye turned to the big blond boy who must have been sitting in the dark corner of the vehicle, because up to now I'd not seen him. The screw whose name was to turn out to be Woodward, slowly came to stand in front of Jansenn.

'What did you do? Jansenn.

Woodward was not quite as tall as the big blond, and was forced to look up at him. The fifteen-year-old seemed to have the look of an old man in his face as he looked down at Woodward.

'Murder.'

Woodward's eyes flickered, but he said nothing.

'Why aren't you in a Borstal?

A Borstal was a closed institution that resembled more of a high security prison. Bars, barbed wire, searchlights and dogs.

The blond shrugged his shoulders.

'Who did you kill?'

'My Father.'

A pin dropping to the floor would have sounded like an earthquake, I was holding my breath without realising it, my pulse hammering in my ears.

'What for?'

'He beat my mother.'

The cane reached out and tapped the big blond on the chest.

'When you talk to me or any of the officers here, you will say sir. Understand!'

With an ease that surprised me and everyone present, the big blond took the cane and broke it in two.

'I only say 'sir' to my father. Touch me once more with that stick and I'll ram it down your throat.'

The big hands dropped the stick on the floor, and Woodward stepped back a pace, his face white, hand shaking as he lifted a whistle to his mouth.

The shrill blast seemed to exho down long corridors and reverberate back to the front door. There was a sound of many heavy booted feet approaching from different directions. Six or seven heavily built men pounded into the entrance hall. Woodward stepped back, his face white.

'Take him to solitary. I'll deal with him later.'

But the big blond didn't go easily. His fist fell and rose as the men suddenly tried to pin him against the wall, from somewhere in the melee came the sound of bone breaking. A scream, and then heavy voices and panting. I watched breathless as the blond was dragged away, his big feet leaving a rubber trail on the highly polished floor. I had been frightened before, but this was more than I'd ever expected. I was watching something . . . no . . . I was part of something which was untrue . . . the sheer brutality frightened me. I had to breathe deep many times to be able to control my nerves . . . I was only thankful I was not the only one affected by what had happened. Woodward had to take a few deep breaths before he could speak.

'In a few . . . in a few minutes . . . the Governor will be seeing you. If he addresses you, you answer with your name and sentence. If the Governor is kind enough . . . kind enough . . .'

Woodward was still trying to get over the shock . . . it was a fact I found interesting.

'. . . to ask you a question, you will answer yes or no . . . Understand? But nothing more, say anything you're not asked and I'll have your guts for garters.'

'Yes, sir.'

We answered in unison, nobody wanted to feel the wrath of this man anymore.

The Governor was a grey haired stately sort of man, and it seemed hard to believe he had men such as Woodward working for him. He came around his desk and sat on the edge of it. Studied us for a few minutes and then addressed us in a soft voice. He always seemed to be smiling.

'My name is Bradley and I am the Governor here. For those of you who are first timers, I'll explain the purpose of the place that you're at. This is a remand and assessment centre. None of you will be staying here, you will be sent to other remand places which best suit you and your situation. That is the purpose of you being here, to assess what is best for your rehabilitation back into society.

The sentences that you've been given are the maximum time that you can serve if you behave yourselves . . . the time can also be shortened if you show that you have learnt your lesson. For any of you who have a minimum sentence to be served, for example three years, then I'm sorry, but the best thing you can do is to settle down and hope the three years goes quickly. But for the rest of you, how much time you serve is up to you. We have no wish to keep you away from your families any longer than necessary. But you have to learn that if you break the law, then there is a penalty to pay for it.

'We shall try to pick an approved school which is convenient for your parents to visit. But we also have to look at your abilities and future requirements; if the school you're sent to is hundreds of miles from your home . . . then it's because its the best for you.

'Now, in a moment Mr Woodward will take you away from here . . . by the way . . . Mr Woodward is the head warder here . . . and will issue you with school clothes and a locker that you can keep the odd one or two personal items. Any money you have will have to be handed in for safe keeping. You'll be issued with a number whilst you are here, that number will be your identification. Should your number appear on a notice board then you are to contact the duty officer. Should any of you have any problems here or at home, then for goodness sake, contact the duty officer instead of trying to escape from here and sort the problem out yourself.

'Our day starts at six in the morning, we do a little house cleaning, breakfast at seven thirty, lunch at twelve thirty, tea at four thirty and supper at eight. Bed and lights out at nine o'clock. Any questions?' We looked at each other but no one had forgotten the presence of Woodward. The Governor got to his feet and walked towards his large window that overlooked a pleasant garden. He stopped and clasped his hands behind his back, then turned half towards us as if he'd forgotten a tiny unimportant detail.

'Oh, yes. There is one small thing I forgot to tell you. All the doors in this building are locked day and night. All the windows are barred and any attempt to escape will be severely dealt with. The holding of any escape material will be considered as an attempt to escape. There have been few who've managed to get away from here and make a successful escape. The local Police are by now quite expert at catching anyone who escapes. The punishment for escaping is six lashes of the cane across both hands, loss of all privileges for fourteen days, plus thirty days on your time ... for each attempt. Three attempts and you go into a borstal, which is more like a maximum security prison. It's better to be happy here until you get to your permanent place ... after all ... it's more like home here.'

He turned away and looked at the garden, it was our dismissal.

'About turn. Quick march. Left right left right ...'

We tramped out of the office, and down a succession of long narrow corridors, stopping for numerous doors to be unlocked and locked again as we went through them. Finally we reached a large room that was lined with knee high wooden lockers. It didn't take long to realise that the multitude of locks on some of the lockers were to prevent others from stealing the contents. These were the private lockers assigned to every boy in the place. Another screw came through a locked door at the end of the room and joined Woodward.

'All right you lot. Empty everything out of your pockets and put it down on the table.'

The other boys stepped forward and took a great assortment of stuff from their pockets and placed it on the large table in front of them, their eyes flicking back and forwards, guarding their possessions.

'What's wrong with you, Dawson. Have you gone deaf?'

'I don't have anything, sir.'

Woodward grunted and took a handful of large envelopes from his colleague.

'Write your names and home addresses on the envelopes. Take your clothes off and fold them in a neat pile on the table. In a moment we'll tell each of you what you can keep and what will have to go back to your parents. Anybody with money, put it on the table and it will be entered into a book against your name. Your clothes will be parcelled up and sent back to your parents. Where you're going you won't be needing them for a long time. Then you'll take a very hot, disinfectant shower and either Matron or the Doctor will inspect you for fleas, scurvy, lice or whatever else. Then you'll be issued with a school uniform. Any questions?'

The look on his face said he wasn't in the slightest bit interested to hear our questions.

'Right. Undress, shower and examination, then back here. And I don't want to hear a sound from anyone. M-O-V-E.'

I was never to know exactly what happened then. But suddenly the boy next to me began to shout at me, for what seemed to be no reason whatsoever. Woodward was around the table and taking a handful of my hair in his hand, before I could even raise a word of protest. My head felt like it was coming apart as he pulled me down. The cane came down unmercifully on my backside, until I thought I couldn't take any more. My lungs were tortured for air, and this time there was no point in holding back the tears. I was bent over backwards nearly double trying to ease the pain in my backside.

'I can see you're a troublemaker, Dawson. We'll soon knock that out of you my lad. You can have a good hiding everyday if you are so disposed. Would have been good for you earlier, perhaps you wouldn't be here now.'

I could almost feel the blood running from my teeth as I gritted them hard together. Such pain I'd never experienced before. At that moment I learnt something new about myself. I would happily kill Woodward if he put another hand on me . . . or any other person . . . if this what life was about, then I had nothing further to lose.

I discovered very quickly that the remand home had two tiers of government. The first one was dictated by the older boys, and enforced rigidly, by any means possible. The second and the most important one was that which was imposed by the screws.

It was also clear that discipline was often overseen by the older boys, because the jailers had a very nasty habit of punishing everybody for something that was done by one person.

The 120 boys in the home where split into four groups, each group being given a house name. This group was again split up into groups of six, according to the tables sitting plan. Each table had someone who was responsible for the rest of those who sat at the table, usually the eldest boy, or one who had been there the longest, or, as sometimes happened the strongest took over. This group was again split, one boy was assigned to lay the table, one appointed to bring the food and another appointed to do the washing up. These duties were rotated every few days, with one table being responsible for washing up and clearing away for the entire house for the week. It requires no further explanation, the system was ready for abuse, and abused it was. The weak were dominted by the strong and the crazy. The best of the food went to the table leader, with the newcomers getting what was left. The best beds went to the strongest whilst the newcomers got the broken ones. When it came to the allocating of cleaning duties, the favoured got work which allowed them as much free time as possible, and the less favoured got the scrubbing duties.

It is inevitable in such a close knit society, where life is governed by fear and violence, that a system or barter comes into operation. And in this place, the barter system was running more smoothly than anything I'd ever seen. For one cigarette you could get someone beaten up in the toilets. For bartering your breakfast for a week you could buy two cigarettes. For giving up a complete lunch you could buy half a box of matches. When matches were scarce, then one lunch would perhaps purchase one match expertly cut into four pieces. Smoking by the way . . . was forbidden, but it was the currency of any form of trade within the remand home. Nothing could be bought or traded without tobbaco, tobbaco papers or matches being involved. Those who had the currency were the powerful ones, those without it had to suffer in silence. How did the supplies get into the remand home? It was brought in by the world-wise parents, who already knew a thing or two about the system which operated in such places.

We were introduced to a fat motherly woman who had a permanent smile on her face.

'Hello, boys. My name is Mrs Wooley, better known as the Laundry Woman. My job is to look after your clothes, and see that they are in good repair, and to issue you with fresh clothes each week.'

I found myself liking the woman. But another side of my brain was screaming extreme caution in handling my emotions, it could just be another trick to lull me into a false sense of security. I began to listen to what my brain was telling me, after all, each time I'd exposed my emotions to someone, they'd crushed me, and painfully. I looked at the woman with

different eyes now, suddenly the smile hid the diamond hard
eyes shining through the rolls of fat. The fat pudgy hands
looked like they were capable of squeezing my neck like they
would squeeze the juice out of an orange. I listened to what
else she had to say.

'I hope you'll understand that because of your short stay
here, we can't issue everyone of you with new clothes. The
clothes which you receive have been worn by other boys before
you, and will be worn by others who will come here after you,
so treat the clothes with care. Now if you make a line in front
of me, I can issue you with your remand number and clothes.
When you've had your shower and inspection, I want you to
leave your civilian clothes outside where later on we can get
them washed and sent back to your parents. By the time you'll
need those clothes, you're going to be too big to wear them.'

The smile deepened, but this time I wasn't taken in by it.
The psychological terror behind the words wasn't missed on
me either. She was telling us we were going to be a long time
'inside.'

When it came to my turn to receive the prison number and
the clothes assigned to it, she looked at me with shrewd eyes,
and then at the clothes I was wearing.

'My, young man. Whatever we give you is going to be much
better than what you're wearing now. Where have you come
from?'

'Erdington.'

The smile went a bit crooked.

'Silly boy. What I meant, is what sort of home have you
come from. What you're wearing looks like a school uniform
. . . though more than somewhat worn out. And those boots
you have on . . . they must be about three sizes too big for
you.'

I looked down at the big curled up toes of the boots.
Suddenly the boots did look rather oversized against the thin
sticks of legs that were showing out of the top of them. I
looked at the patches on my grey shorts and had to admit that
against the other boys there with me, I did look something like
a street urchin. Strange . . . I'd never noticed it before.
Suddenly I was embarrassed.

'I was in a foster home.'

'But surely they could dress you better than that . . .'

Suddenly she turned away and took a pile of clothes from a pigeon hole on the wall, then thrust them into my hands.

'Your number is seventy-three, imprint the number in your brain. Forget it, and you'll have problems. And do try to take better care of these clothes.'

The smile was still on the face, but I'd heard that type of words too often to be taken in any more, this woman was no better than my foster mother.'

It seemed to take hours to go through all the de-civilising formalities. Clothes gone, possessions gone. Anything of value taken away. Haircut almost to the skin. Learning to walk in a line behind each other, never speaking, keep the eyes to the ground. Showering, medical inspection. Upstairs to make our own beds according to the rules and regulations laid down. Then back downstairs and standing in a line. Name and address of parents. Religion. School qualifications. Father's job.

Slowly, oh so slowly, I felt myself sink further and further away from the world outside. I was being dehumanized, nothing was allowed to lie secret within my breast. The voices droned on, stripping and chipping away at all those secret little things which made human beings out of us. Until there was nothing left for them to learn, then we all turned like zombies and shuffled after the warder who was leading us to the dining room.

120 hostile heads turned towards us as the subdued hubub of voices suddenly ceased. Each face went through a kaleidoscope of emotions from, searching for a friend, looking for a friendly face, to open hostility in case their position in the prison hierarchy might be threatened. There was also hostility when it meant that five people at a table enjoying food for six, might suddenly have to give up the extra rations to feed another one. The hostility in the room was naked, and I felt as if I'd walked into the lion's den.

As soon as I had sat at the table which was appointed to me, I knew there would be trouble between me and the table leader.

He was someone who ruled by fear, and believed in the power of force. The other boys at the table were just . . . faces . . . such was this one boy's dominance. The look on his face was supposed to portray to me what no words could define . . .

I'm the boss of this table. Knowing that no matter what I did or said there would be trouble, I decided to jump in at the deep end.

A fork jammed my hand down on the table, it's prongs digging deeper and deeper into the flesh. I slowly looked up at the snarling face of the table leader, his lips drawn back over his teeth, voice low so as not to be overheard.

'On this table you don't touch any food until I tell you to.'

The other four faces at the table were now looking down at their plates ... I was on my own.

The fork suddenly dug deeper into the back of my hand and I had to grit my teeth hard so as not to cry out.

'Do you understand? ... or shall we go for a little walk to the 'Bogs' afterwards.'

I had come to realise sometime ago that my life was not worth anything to anyone, not even to myself, especially when I was so powerless to control events in it. But this ... this was something which I could control. This was the lowest form of civilised behaviour ... and yet it was ... the highest. Whatever I did now, would have a very serious effect on my position within this closed society ... and I was excruciatingly aware of that fact. Here, only the power of barter and the fear of violence was the currency by which all things were measured.

I looked steadily at the eyes across the table, and could feel the distinct unease of the other boys. This was a power struggle, and already they were thinking about their own survival ... should they come down on my side ... or stay with the devil they knew. Each one of them was painfully aware of what happened in the 'Bogs'. It was the place where the high court of such a society took place.

The 'Bogs' were the toilets, a place where the trials and judgements were carried out according to the school's unwritten laws. The screws knew about the practise, but always turned a blind eye to it ... it was a very necessary evil to keep the system going. I was almost at the point of giving in as the points of the fork dug deeper into the skin, the pain almost beyond the point of containment ... when the hand flashed back and the boy sat smiling at me ... how could I see one of the screws approaching the table from behind.

'What's your name?'

'Dawson . . . sir.'

'Why aren't you eating?'

'Errr . . . I was just thinking about what to eat.'

I saw the man's eyes fall to the empty soup terrine and my clean plate.

'Where's his soup?'

The look of innocence on the table leader's face was a total contrast to what I'd seen a few seconds before.

'I'm sorry, sir. But there was only enough for the five of us. The kitchens must have forgotten that a new boy would be coming.'

The officer thought about it for a moment, it was plain to see he was wondering whether to believe it or not. The other faces at the table turned to look at him and nodded their support to the statement. They had survived another power struggle, and come down on the side of he who at that moment held the crown.

'All right. I'll talk to the kitchen and tell them to make up another setting.'

As the man disappeared I saw the table leader nod his head at the boy who was sat on my left in the line of succession. There was a very painful kick in the leg from the heavy shoes which almost brought tears to my eyes.

'Be thankful you didn't say anything, or else he would have cut your throat.'

I tried sucking air into my tortured lungs as I looked at the table leader. This was only the beginning.

When I reached the dormitory that evening, I felt my heart drop to my boots realising that my table leader was also in the bed next to mine.

'So. I not only have you on my table, I've also got you next to me . . . I don't like you.'

I had to swing around to look at him, the tone of voice rang alarm bells in my head . . . his eyes were staring almost sightlessly at me . . . he was unpredictable . . . he was . . . crazy.

I quickly turned back to my bed, busying myself in the hope that he would become disinterested. The young man frightened me with his far away look in the eyes. I was locked away in a place where society's rules and regulations couldn't get in. No one in this place seemed the slightest bit interested in what was happening around them, but they were extremely aware of each other's weaknesses with a clarity that was frightening. And they protected their small private area of the world with ruthless brutality.

'I don't like you . . .'

He was out to make trouble . . . nasty trouble at that. I quickly looked around me, but it was as if the rest of the boys in the dormitory were deaf. There was no one who was about to step in and save the situation. I knew, if I wasn't careful then the situation was going to deteriorate into an all out life and death brawl.

'Err . . . look . . . I'm sorry. I certainly didn't . . .'

'I don't like you . . .'

The voice was calm, frighteningly calm. The eyes were almost unseeing . . . the air was filled with an electrical charge . . . and the rest of the boys were moving surreptitiously around their beds to put as much distance between us as possible. This alone was unnerving as I was facing an unknown quantity. What did they know about him that made them behave in such a way . . . was he violent? . . . was he dangerous? There was certainly something about him that made those around very nervous. I carefully tried to place the bed between him and me without giving him the impression I was running away . . . which was exactly what I was doing.

I barely had time to get my feet out of the way as he grabbed my bed and turned it over, the mattress and blankets flying across the highly polished wooden floor, the iron bed frame clattering to the boards. He advanced with a devastating determination, and I knew if he caught me it would be all up, he wouldn't stop until there was a corpse at his feet. My fear of him, and of the rest of the boys, began to put a band of steel into my yellow spine. If this was the way that I had to go, then so be it . . . I would take him with me. Once the decision had been made, a great calm descended over me. With a precision I had not realised I possessed, I waited for him to advance on me until there was only the thickness of the upturned bed between us, then pummelled him unmercifully until a dozen hands fell on me and dragged me away. I was aware of nothing that went on around me, only the burning desire to kill this boy . . . before he killed me.

The blow seared the skin of my face as the hard, work

seasoned hand hammered my head from side to side.

'Take him to solitary confinement. We'll soon teach him a lesson.'

I had known nothing of the screw turning up in the dormitory. He'd seen my bed overturned and scattered across the floor, and had seen me beating the hell out of another boy . . . only hours after arriving in the remand home . . . I was to learn that justice in such a place came with a vengeance.

I struggled against the eager hands which were dragging me down long corridors to some unknown destination. I received sly kicks and punches from boys who were enjoying themsleves for a few minutes of legalised brutality. They dragged and carried me by different parts of my anatomy, accompanied by laughs and grunts to a cell which was set into a solid structure of bricks, mortar, and lots of reinforced concrete, and a massive steel and wood door.

I was dropped unceremoniously on the floor, to the accompaniment of heavy kicks and the last punches before the door closed with a finality which nearly burst the ear drums with the sudden and utter silence . . . it was a padded cell.

Before I had got my wits about me, the door was again flung open and a very irate warden stood in front of me, behind him another screw with a cane in his hands. I struggled to my feet with some effort, every joint and limb aching from the beating as I'd been dragged here. The warden's voice was shaking with the suppressed anger.

'You've been here barely a few hoours, and in that time you've upset most of this remand home, and hospitalised one of it's inmates. Such behaviour will not be tolerated in my remand home. According to the rules laid down for the running of this establishment, your act of wanton violence will cost you an extra month of time on your sentence, twelve strokes of the cane and three days solitary confinement with bread and water, and thirty minutes of exercise each day. Plus a loss of all priviliges for the next thirty days.'

He stepped back, two screws pushed past him and launched themselves at me. They were burly men, men who were employed more for their ability to be rough than for the brains in their heads. One trapped me against the wall with all 200 pounds of his body, his broad hands yanking my hands away from my body and holding them out for the other man who wielded the cane with all the force he could muster. The cane crashed into the bones of my hands, the crushing blows first numbing and then bringing enormous waves of pain which swept through the body until my brain screamed out in silent agony. I hardly knew anything about being pinned face to the wall and receiving further blows across the backside, my brain was in such shock from the intense pain, it viewed everything from the security of semi-consciousness.

Whilst the world rushed into the Swinging Sixties, laughing, wining and dining on the vast amounts of money that floated on a bouyant market, pledging never to wage war again and to wipe out all brutality with lots of happiness; I opened my eyes and was amazed to find I was still alive.

It took a moment or two to realise I really was alive, the realisation coming as I tried to use my hands to raise my aching body to it's knees.

Pain eminated from every pore as my body came alive to the lingering shocks from the caning. I couldn't use my hands to support my weight, they felt as though they were swollen out of all proportion. And as I used my legs, the skin across my lower back and backside ached from every movement. I felt as though an army had walked across my body, and suddenly I collapsed on the mattress as the last of my strength left the battered frame.

Even to this day, thirty years later, I'm unable to tell how long I lay there trying to summon the strength to get up from the floor of that padded cell. The silence was so total, so devastatingly total, that I hardly knew where the floor, the ceiling, or the walls were.

How long it took me to realise that the world I was in was totally dark, I shall never know. But I can remember well the moment a very strong light was put on in the ceiling, forcing me to cover my eyes as I cowered against the wall . . . I was sure the next beating was not far away.

The sounds of the world came at me with a shattering volume of noise as the door was opened. Laughing voices, stern commands, rattling of far off keys floated into my dungeon of silence as the man I recognised as being the doctor, stood in the doorway.

'Is your name Dawson?'

It surprised me just how difficult it was to croak out the answer. My throat was dry and hoarse, and as I moved my mouth I could feel the dried salt on my cheeks . . . I had cried . . . the cry of the damned.

'Ye . . . es.'

'I can't hear you.'

I cleared my throat with difficulty. My voice feeling a little stronger.

'Yes.'

The man was stern and authoritarian, he somehow failed to live up to the picture I had always had in my mind about doctors.

'Stand in the middle of the cell. Turn around, drop your trousers and bend over.'

The world had so few surprises left for me, that I wouldn't have been surprised if the doctor was going to give me a further beating. I stumbled into the middle of the cell and did as was ordered, my eyes screwed up against the expected blows. But none came.

All I could hear was a sharply indrawn breath.

'Stand up. Pull up your trousers and show me your hands.'

The effort required to make my swollen hands perform the more difficult task of buttoning my trousers, was evidently not lost on the doctor.

'Does it hurt?'

I didn't know what to answer. If I said yes, someone, somewhere, was bound to get into trouble. If I said no, then I would have to suffer the consequences . . . either way. I had learnt in my foster home to take what comes and if you are silent it is over a little quicker. I didn't answer and he asked no more questions.

The rest of the examination was carried out with professional thoroughness and then he pronounced me fit to serve the sentence of three days solitary confinement on a diet of bread and water. My sentence started the moment he pronounced me fit, only God knew how long I had already been in the cell . . . I certainly didn't.

As the door closed, I looked down at the three pieces of dried bread and the plastic jug of water that had been left behind. I looked and looked at it until the edges curled up, and the total silence slowly sucked the life from my soul. The tears ran down my face, but there was only the padded walls to pluck the sounds of my cries from the air. I laid down on the mattress and slowly curled up into a foetal position and wished to all the gods known, that they would take my life.

When the door was finally opened at the end of the third day, I realised I had experienced the most brutal of all punishments known to man. The total and absolute shutting off of all form of contact to the world that you are born into. I had experienced seventy-two hours of silence . . . enforced silence . . . where even the sound of life was plucked from the air before your ears could hear it. I had experienced the dizzying stomach churning shock when I realised that not even the boys who walked past the tiny window which was set in the heavy door, could hear me pounding on the structure. I had shouted and screamed at them, but I could have whispered for all the good it did me.

I had experienced the nauseating feeling of realising I was nothing to this world except a number on a piece of paper, to be manipulated and moved around life's chessboard according to the whims of those who felt the need to exercise their power. But most of all I had experienced untold hours of terror . . . my imagination running wild as I thought about the possibility of being forgotten in this cell. I'd had nightmares when I'd forced the hours to pass in sleep, nightmares where I'd seen myself pounding the door whilst the rest of the inmates passed by as they left me in a deserted building. The sweat had run freely as the nightmares had been dragged out, and even to this day I cannot bear someone else shutting doors against me.

The purity of the thousand different sounds which flooded my ears, sounds which I'd never been aware of before, made me finally realise I was still alive, and living in a very noisy world. And as I marched down the long corridor behind the screw who had let me out, I realised I'd gained a new status and much respect in the three days I'd been in the cell. Some boys just smiled, others gave me a thumbs up sign, others cowered against the wall as I passed, and some avoided my eyes. I'd gone into the cell as just one of a number, but now I was returning to the world with my status and position assured within this bone hard society that existed on the edge of hell.

★   ★   ★   ★

I was to be in this remand home for exactly two weeks, and in these two weeks I was to learn an awful lot about my fellow travellers.

There was an atmosphere in the air of mutual conspiracy against those whose job it was to keep you incarcerated. It was an unwritten rule that nobody volunteered information to the jailers which could in anyway be used to lengthen the stay of anyone. It was also an unwritten rule that anyone who offended against the unwritten rules was to accept their punishment like a man . . . in other words, to stay quiet. Softness, or running behind the backs of the jailers and whispering to them was the equivalent of committing a capital crime in a normal society, and anyone suspected of or being found out of such an act could expect to be summarily punished . . . very painfully, and to be banished from all activities and from the protective umbrella of the unit. The jailers where quick to spot anyone who had been banned, and did their best to get them sent to another establishment as soon as possible.

When I'd got over the initial shock of being confined to a building surrounded by steel bars and locked doors, I took a long look at my situation.

For the next three years I would never again be allowed to walk in any direction I chose. It would always be in the highly restricted and confined area designated by my jailers. The extent of my freedom would be measured by how long it would take me to walk from one locked door to another, accompanied by the inevitable jailer with his badge of authority hanging from a chain on his belt . . . the keys . . . without their keys most of the jailers would have been no different to the rest of us. They were often helping themselves to food or whatever was lying around, taking it to their homes to help supplement their meagre salaries.

What did hurt most, was the fact I was not allowed to look out of the windows. It was strictly forbidden to cast an eye on the outside world through the odd one or two windows which were placed at a level to be looked through. This was a particularly brutal part of the punishment in such an establishment, because again, it created a privilege which was fought and bartered for.

There were three places in the remand home which had a window which could be looked out of: the dormitory, on the top floor; the assessment room, on the ground floor; and the day room, also on the ground floor. Incarcerating the body is not nearly so bad if the eyes can see the outside world. But when the mind is also incarcerated, then it begins to look inward and shrinks to the size of the world it is forced to live in. Even at our tender age, we'd become painfully aware of the value to our souls and our memories of far places and loved ones that a glimpse . . . no matter how short . . . of the outside world meant. When you saw the sun glancing from the tall buildings of the far away city of Birmingham . . . when you saw the greens of the trees momentarily lit up before the cloud crossed the sun . . . when you saw birds flying freely across the sky . . . then you knew you were still part of the world and for a while you daydreamed on a plain far above those around you. Even now, I have great difficulty staying in a room without windows . . . windows that I can see the world from . . . windows from which I can see far horizons.

Knowing all this, a position by the window was jealously fought for when we were allowed into anyone of the above places. The position could be bartered for huge sums of the establishment's staple currency . . . cigarettes and matches. Those who were either too poor to have the means to barter, or were too soft to fight, would survive for days on the descriptions given by someone who had had a glimpse . . . of . . . of . . .

The assessment room was the place where everybody had to go at least once during his stay. It was a room where each person was forced to sit and go through an examination to assess the full extent of his schooling and general knowledge. It was also the room which had the largest window in the building, overlooking the far away spires of Birmingham. When the so called 'Government experts' made their assessments of the criminal mind, they should have at least had the intelligence not to carry out the examination in rooms that gave a view on the outside world. Papers were continually messed up, so the test would have to be rewritten, and suddenly even the most intelligent found it difficult to spell or do even the most basic of sums . . . which led to having to spend even more time in the assessment room. Even though the window was at our backs, it didn't stop the lucky two sitting next to it from getting drunk on the view.

It was in the dormitory that power and strength obtained a place by the window. At least once a month, the position was fought for by anybody who felt strong enough to challenge those already in place. When the present occupant of the most favoured place was sent on to his long term place of detention, his bed would be eyed jealously by all those around him. Sometimes he himself would appoint his successor, who would also automatically become the leader of the remand homes secret hierarchy, or he would allow the position to fall free as his mind became more and more occupied by the imminent move to his new place of detention and a new struggle for his position within a much more established system.

The window in the dormitory was the most favoured place because it was the only window in the entire building which could be opened or closed, even the few centimetres allowed, at will by whoever slept by it . . . if they chose to sleep. Often they could be seen late into the night, sitting on the end of their bed, looking through the glass at the lights of the faraway city . . . dreaming with their eyes open.

Every day started with the same routine. Each member of the remand home was appointed a job by his table leader, who incidentally came under the baleful eye of the one who occupied the bed under the window.

Floors and passageways had to be scrubbed on hands and knees, with buckets of freezing water. Wooden floors had to be swept and polished, whilst door handles were polished until they gleamed. The cleaning of the entrance hall, and the front step, and door handles was a privilege given by the 'Boss.'

That such a system was allowed to exist, was a measure of the jailers' acknowledgement that the system they operated was far from perfect . . . a long way from perfect. We were forced to exist like wild animals in cages, each one fighting to the best of his abilities to gain even the most meagre advantage over those around him.

The jobs would be handed out according to one's standing within the society. The dirtiest job in the remand centre was the cleaning of the toilets, something which could turn a sensitive stomach. If anyone had offended the unwritten rules of the place, then he could be sure that the next day he would be cleaning the toilets out. If there had been a power struggle overnight, then the toppled leader would be seen cleaning the toilets . . . or even scrubbing out the dustbins next day . . . and the jailers would be warned of impending trouble. They knew well that the place couldn't survive without the unchallenged leadership of the strongest.

The most sought after jobs, which could earn large amounts of tobacco and matches in bribes to obtain the jobs, was the kitchens and the cleaning of the entrance hall.

The entrance hall job actually meant going outside the building, with a jailer of course, to scrub the stone steps and glass door with it's ornate brass handles. It meant that someone could go outside and experience for an hour or more the heady feeling of unlimited space and fresh air. They could feel the warmth of the early morning sun on their white skin, and listen to the birds singing . . . and feel their souls expand from that life giving atmosphere.

The kitchens was also a favoured job. Everybody suffered from permanent hunger, some more than others. Working in the kitchens meant that you stole food for your friends, or for barter. A job in the kitchen meant you suddenly realised how many friends you had, when you didn't even know they existed before. Sometimes a job in the kitchen was appointed arbitrarily by the jailers from amongst a group of newcomers, and suddenly the lucky one would find himself getting a bed on the right or left of the 'Boss'. Sometimes . . . though rarely . . . he who was chosen to work in the kitchen . . . became the 'Boss'. Then tables would find themselves short of food and others favoured with more, according to the requirements and needs of the Boss.

Because of my special status, of having survived a brutal beating and three days bread and water in solitary confinement without uttering a single word of complaint, it brought me the special privilege of being allowed to sit on the Boss's table.

It was here that I was to learn what a privilege such as that meant. The Boss's table was where the events and happenings of the remand centre were discussed, each occupant of the table went to make up the unofficial governing body of the place. The Boss's table was also favoured with sufficient food.

If someone had offended the code, then during the meal

hour it would be discussed and a suitable punishment would be chosen and passed on. The punishment would be carried out by one of those who moved continually around the Boss waiting for favours to be bestowed upon them; establishing their own position within the hierarchy without having to fight for it.

It was a measure of the psychological instability of those who were appointed to run such establishments, that often they created situations which they were supposed to prevent.

One incident occured that I'll always remember, not because of what happened, but because of the sadistic mind that built the event to such dangerous levels.

One has to imagine the wide ranging characters that it needs to inhabit such a place as a remand and assessment centre. The wild, unstable, untamed. The violent, the scared, the crazy, the lost . . . and those who should never ever have been put into such a place. They are young . . . not younger than eleven and no older than about eighteen. 120 young men and boys, going through puberty, mixed up, unsure of themselves, scared to death of showing any morsel of weakness, but one thing binds them together . . . they each have a family and loved ones on the outside . . . and a boy's ties to his family were inviolate.

There had been a postal strike in Birmingham that had lasted for more than four days. The strike had resulted in a total stoppage of all mail to the centre. Nobody . . . not one single person . . . had received news from the outside world.

Even though the letters were always opened and read by the jailers, and even whole sections cut out of the letters with a pair of scissors, the letters . . . sometimes even just the envelopes were handed out by the lunchtime duty screw. Then at least those who were inside knew that they had not been forgotten by those outside.

When there is a delay in receiving the mail for a few days, there is a perceptable tension that begins to grow. The inmates begin to lose contact with the basic laws of society as tensions grow and flare-ups occur over even the most trivial of incursions into ones own private little world. It is with this in mind, this feeling of being cut off from the outside world, lost, nothing more to lose, not wanted, that we approach the end of the mid-day meal one day.

The meal was being finished and some of the tables had begun clearing away the dishes. The duty jailer was walking around the dining hall, hands behind his back, an aura of impatience and sadistic pleasure eminating from him.

We . . . that is the inmates . . . being treated like animals had developed the instincts of animals and could each one feel the malevolence of this man. We were all painfully aware of the fact that he could choose . . . or not choose as was his want . . . to hand out the mail once the meal was over and the dining room was absolutely silent. Something which was absolutely rare for 120 boys and young men. It was a moment that the jailers would taunt the inmates unmercifully, settling some personal vendetta, or satisfying some sadistic urge within themselves . . . glorying in the absolute power they had over their charges.

Tensions were beginning to build within the dining room as 120 pairs of eyes had been eyeing the unusually large pile of letters which had been lying on a podium against the far wall. The jailer knew he wouldn't have to say a word, the room would fall silent on it's own. And he would wait . . . he would savour the pleasure of that moment as he demanded the impossible from them . . . absolute silence.

There was a cough, the jailer put down the letter he had lifted and calmly looked at the occupants of the room. Five days they had been without mail, they were nervous, hungry for news from home, they were like predatory animals. The strained silence hung in the air as the jailer slowly lifted the first letter . . . a chair moved nervously and there was a whimper from someone who was holding his emotions under a tight reign. The letter was put down . . . deliberately slowly . . . the clock was ticking away . . . it would be almost the end of the appointed time for mail distribution . . . they would have to wait for the following day.

Again the letter was slowly lifted, the room thick with tension . . . someone coughed. The letter was put down and suddenly the air was rent with a wild scream as someone flew across the table tops and began stabbing the boy who had coughed with a blunt knife in the neck. All hell broke loose as inmate fought inmate, and the jailers came in to break it up. The mail was stopped for a further three days because of the uncontrolled violence, and the entire place lived on a knife's edge. Animal circled animal, teeth bared, each one sniffing the intentions of the other, calculating the risk to their safety and that one goal . . . the mail.

It was at times like this I could only sit back and feel sick and lost. I knew there would never ever be a mail call for me, because there was no one out there who even knew I'd existed. I would watch the emotions within each of the inmates as their names were called out and they would get up with shaking legs to collect their letter. I wished I could experience these emotions, know their passions, to feel their warmth, to feel that bond which ties you to someone who cares, to feel that dizzying spiral of love wrap around you when you receive that letter written by them especially for you . . . I would be denied that emotion. Instead I would sit on the sidelines and watch the routine which never ever changed.

When someone received a letter, he would quickly scan it for anything important and then go to some private corner and sit on the floor to devour the letter word by word . . . letter by letter. When the letter had been read ten or fifteen times, they would sit in silence, lost in their own thoughts. The mail was sacrosanct, if anyone dropped his letter, it was never read by anyone else, but handed back to the owner . . . untouched.

Weekends were the only time the place seemed to shake off the shackles of the rigidly laid down rules and relax . . . just a little. It was the time when the place was staffed by the smallest number of wardens, who relied upon the inmates self governing system to keep law and order.

On average, there would be four wardens to supervise the 120 inmates compared to the weekdays when there would be maybe twenty.

It was one weekend of the month when this rule was changed, and that was on visiting day. On this day, there would be six wardens, the extra two being needed to supervise the families of the inmates. But even the visits were surrounded by danger. To enable a visit to take place, the inmate concerned had to apply to one of the wardens for permission to have a visitor. If the warden concerned had no personal reasons for the visit not to take place, then he would submit the application to the Governor who would usually accept the application if it had worked it's way through the system without a problem. Then the inmate was informed of the decision and he could then write home asking his family to visit him.

It was rare that anyone was allowed to have a visitor who was not family or close friend, so every application which was made would have to go through the vetting system. There was an approved list of visitors which was held in the Governors office, anyone who was not on the list, didn't get the permission.

If, between the visiting days, an inmate who had been given permission to have a visit got into trouble, then it was possible for the visit to be cancelled by the Governor acting on advice from the head warden. And the inmate would only learn about it on the day of the visit. Such were the hopes and fears built up during this time, that it in itself created problems.

The visit would always result in the inmate receiving food, cigarettes, money, sweets, and a whole army of approved items which could later be used as bartering material. Even though the items were supposed to be handed over to the staff for safekeeping and rationed handing out, it was inevitable some of it would never be recorded. It would just disappear before the wardens got their hands on it. So the loss of a visit not only deprived someone of contact with the family, it also stripped him of any bartering material until the next visit. Anyone who had nothing to barter with, was in a very bad position.

And so it was, that on this day, if one had survived the three weeks without losing the visiting privilege, the inmates would tread carefully so as not to anger the wardens and have their visit cancelled with a telephone call at the last minute.

It was also on this day that the work allocation would be recklessly given out against the promise of a packet of cigarettes, or bars of chocolate, some favourite food, or even money at the last resort. The most favoured job being the outside working detail.

But, if at the end of the day the debt had not been paid to satisfaction, then justice was swift. It would be a forced visit to the toilets where a severe beating took place, then your head would be pushed into a toilet pan and peed on by the aggreived inmate and the toilet flushed. Rarely was a debt defaulted.

After the big weekend inspection by the wardens to check that all was clean, the staff would be severely reduced and everyone was left to amuse himself as he saw fit. The Saturday afternoon visits created an excitement and expectation within the establishment which made governing it a lot easier.

First everyone had to take a shower in the long shower room which could accommodate up to forty at a time. Then there would be long lines of inmates waiting naked, except for a towel around their waist sometimes in the freezing cold, for the duty warden to inspect them to see that they were clean. No matter what was done within this place, it created problems, problems which could have been easily avoided by treating the inmates with even the most basic semblence of human decency. Fights would occur in the long lines waiting for inspection, because someone wanted to get out of the cold. Or someone was exercising his authority, or someone would promise any number of cigarettes to get near the head of the line. And those who had nothing to barter with, got angrier and angrier as they saw the line get longer and they no nearer to the head of it.

Nothing, but nothing, could get done without the inmate being reduced to the lowest form of animal, with the strongest always fighting to maintain even the slightest dignity over those around him.

Not all those in the place received a visit, most, but not quite all. I was one of those unfortunates who would sit on the floor, back against the wall, watching the excitement mounting as each name was called out and told to go to the day room. I would sit there with the three or four others, secretly praying for my name to be called out, and yet fearing it would, because suddenly I would have to face the reality of the world. How would the visitor see us. Did we still look normal? Had we changed and begun to look like the animals we felt we were? How would we cope with the shock of having a visitor? Would we be able to face the shattering silence afterwards? Would the visitor bring the world crashing into our lives? We so much prayed that someone would call out our names, and yet lived in fear of it ever happening. We had got so used to not being part of the world, that we couldn't face being reminded what was outside.

The biggest single event that could happen in such a place was the escape. Each day we would expectantly wait for the morning roll call to see if anyone was missing. And when they were, their escape would be the topic for days to come. It would be analysed by everyone who would say they had known about it all the time, and the methods which were employed.

Before I go any further I would like to explain something about an escape.

An escape was not a foolhardy act carried out by lunatics or dangerous persons. It was a very carefully calculated deed carried out by someone of high intelligence who had taken all the facts into consideration and calculated all the risks and the consequences. It was invariably an act of desperation. Desperation borne of ignorance, stupidity, or plain stubbornness on behalf of those whose job it was to watch over us.

The escape was not a spontaneous thing, it was something which built up over a period of time usually because of a domestic problem which those in authority seemed to have no understanding for. Even though we were prisoners, shut away from the world, many of us still had ties to the outside world that were stronger than the fear of retribution from the government. Had many of the escapees been given the chance of a sympathetic hearing earlier, then such situations could have been avoided.

One such case springs easily to mind whilst I was still at the assessment centre and it occured just after the Saturday visit. The full details of which we only learnt about later.

The person in question, whom I shall not name, was a very quiet individual who was liked but treated with much caution. He had been sentenced to three years detention for stabbing his mother's lover with a pitchfork. He'd stabbed the man because one night the man had come to the house drunk, and began to beat his mother. Shortly after he'd been detained letters from home had suddenly stopped coming and he'd become scared for his mother.

Because of what he'd done, the warders were not too keen to listen to anything he had to say, condemning him as a dangerous lunatic. He'd tried to get a meeting with the Governor, but all his requests were turned down by the wardens. And every time he'd tried to send letters to his mother, there was never an answer. Little did he know that nobody had been sending his letters.

But then he'd received a visit from a family friend who told him that his mother was ill, dangerously ill in a hospital. For weeks he had fretted over his decision, knowing full well that none of the staff were prepared to listen to him. His requests to visit his mother had been stonily ignored by warders who seemed to have a personal grudge against this quiet young man.

Then he received a second visit from the family friend who said his mother was asking to see him. His decision was made.

Because of his crime, he was not considered to be dishonest, just dangerous. So therefore he had been given the job of a trustee, which was to clean out the Governor's office, and that of the head warder. As will happen, human nature intervened on his behalf.

One day when he'd gone into the Governor's office, he found the Governor's keys lying on the desk. It took him barely two minutes to find a bar of soap and to make an impression of the master key which opened all the doors inside the building, including the front door. With time and a little patience, he had made a key from wire and wax that held together until he was able to get the front door open. He was found at his mother's bedside at five-thirty in the morning by an irate and suspicious hospital staff. He'd been there for more than six hours.

He had gladly gone into solitary confinement, and then a transfer to a top security detention centre.

His mother . . . she made a remarkable recovery after his visit.

But the reason that a successful escape is so disliked, is that it breeds other escapes. And this time from those who become desperate because the first escape was successful.

Superstition runs rife in such a place, and any would be

escaper immediately brings forward any plans to escape, in the hope of reaping some of the euphoric atmosphere which prevails amongst the inmates; the escape from detention is the lifeblood of such an institution.

The second escape took place twenty four hours after the first, and cost an inexperienced warder his job. He had seen smoke pouring from the boiler room at midnight and had sounded the fire alarm and thrown open the front door. Had he checked the source of the smoke, he would have found a bucket of old greasey kitchen rags smouldering under a slowly burning candle. When the fire drill had been successfully carried out and everybody was standing under a star filled sky, it was found that one of the kitchen workers had escaped during the general rush for the safety of the outside world. That night we retired good-naturedly to vitriolic abuse from out minders.

It was two days later, on the Tuesday, that I was called to the Governor's office and informed I was to be transferred to a permanent place of detention the following morning where I was to serve my three year sentence. I was being sent to Chepstow, a place called Sedbury Park, in South Wales.

The following morning I was singled out by the head warder and taken to the clothes room where I was fully expecting to receive the clothers I had arrived at the detention centre with. Instead, I was fitted out with a complete set of new clothes and shoes; something which overawed me just a little. The warder could obviously see my hesitation.

'There's no mistake. The Governor arranged everything. Now get yourself ready and don't take all day about it.'

When I folded my bedding up for the last time, I realised I was scared, scared of what I was going to, and scared of what I would have to face.

I had breakfast alone in the enormous dining room, envious eyes watching me from outside. Then I was taken to the entrance hall and told to wait. I stood like some lost refugee between two locked doors with a large brown, sealed, envelope in my hand which contained the story of my life.

It was the Governor who opened the door when the bell was rung. Then he turned and looked at me.

'Well, Dawson. I hope you like the clothes my wife bought for you?'

'Yes, thank you, sir.'

'Good. Then off you go, and the best of luck to you. I hope you'll be happy at the place we've picked for you.'

With that the door was closed on me and locked, and suddenly I realised how much I wanted it to be opened and told I could stay there.

'Are you ready to go?'

I turned to face the voice and was faced by a very tall and good looking woman, and for the first time in my life suddenly realised there was another half of the world that existed.

'Err . . . yes . . .'

She saw my hesitation and knew I was having difficulty in addressing her.'

'I am Ann Summers. You can call me 'Miss' or Miss Summers. I'm here to take you to your new place. Do you have everything?'

The question was asked because I was standing there without any personal belongings.

'Yes . . . Miss.'

'No personal items from home . . . or something?'

'No . . . nothing.'

No. I had nothing . . . not even an anchor to hold on to. All that I possessed and all I had been was contained in the file I was clutching to my chest. She sensed her mistake.

I'm sorry.'

There was that smile again. Enchanting and infectious. What had happened to me and the world since the first day the door behind me had been locked on me.

'What's your name?'

'Dawson.'

'Do you have a first name?'

'Geoffrey . . .'

I looked her in the eyes, and suddenly realised that as long as I had a name, I was at least someone.

'All right, Geoffrey. Why don't you call me Ann, until we get to your new place.'

'Yes . . . Miss.'

She saw my hesitation and must have realised I'd never ever had the luxury of talking to someone in familiar terms before. Again that infectious smile.

'If it's easier for you then call me Miss.'

Suddenly I thrust out the file that was in my hands to cover my embarrassment.

'I . . . I was told to give this to you . . . Miss . . . Ann.'

She took the envelope with a slim long fingered hand and then held out her hand to me.

'Would you care to come on a long ride with me. I promise to be good and to make the trip very interesting.'

It seemed so alien for me to hold hands with someone, and had difficulty in taking it. But when those firm fingers wrapped around mine, all hesitation, fears, misgivings or whatever disappeared and I happily walked to her car.

I'd been told I was going to an Approved School in Wales, but my concept of places and distanced hadn't prepared me for this trip.

We seemed to go on for ever, mile after mile, hill after hill, valley after valley. From the heavy industrialised area of Birmingham to the rolling green hills of the countryside. For the very first time in my life I saw cows in a field, and had to ask her to stop the car so I could get out and look at them. This was a different life to the one I knew. There were no street signs to tell you which road you were on, there were no shops, and there was hardly any people around. Where could everyone be? I suddenly turned to her, I had to know the answers.

'Is this detention place in a big city?'

When I looked at her, she seemed too . . . too . . . nice to be my jailer. Again that infectious smile.

'No I'm afraid not. In fact, the nearest city is some forty miles away. But there is a small village about ten miles away.'

I looked around at the vast open spaces which surrounded me, one could get lost out here . . . easily.

'Are you a warden at this detention place?'

Twelve years of very hard, brutal, living had left me devoid of one important thing . . . tact. I saw her wince and wished I hadn't asked the question, she had tried hard to be understanding. But suddenly I wanted her to be the one who at least would tell me the truth . . . just once . . . for someone to be absolutely honest with me, and not to cover everything with a pack of lies.

'I work at the place, yes. But I'm not a . . . warden as you call them. I'm a psychologist. My job is to try and help young men like you with their personal problems.'

For a moment I felt naked, exposed, betrayed. I had begun to open myself to her, I had begun to overcome my fears of people because she had been ... tricking me. She was just another of those damned people who thought they knew more about the way your head operated than you did yourself. She was another of those people who buggered-up the lives of innocent people because they had this quirk inside them which compelled them to interfere in the lives of those THEY thought had problems. I had heard horrific stories in the remand centre of boys who had been sentenced to long prison sentences because of reports which were submitted by people like ... her.

She must have felt my change of mood because she gently turned me to face her, but I refused to look at her.

'What's wrong?'

I didn't want to answer her, to tell her that I'd been stupid enough to ... like her.

'I'd hoped you were something different. But you're no different to the rest of your kind ... I wanted you to be different.'

I'd said it, and now I was sure she would make her own interpretation which would be totally wrong ... again.

'Is it me you don't like? Or is it psychologists you don't like?'

Did it matter what she did to me ... she would have her own opinion ... and mine ... she wouldn't care ... but I wanted her to understand ... at least once.

'The two can't be separated. You are what you are.'

I felt the weight of her arm on my shoulder, and though I tried to force myself not to notice it, the closeness and familiarity had that effect on me ... if she had said run, I would have run till my lungs burst ... just for her.

'Why don't you like psychologists?'

I was so glad she hadn't asked me why I didn't like her.

'Because they're so mixed up. When I'm happy, they say I should be unhappy. When I'm sad, they say I'm selfish. When my whole body is bursting with frustration, they say I'm ungrateful for what's done for me. When I can only cry because the world refuses to listen to me, they say I'm temperamental. When you talk to psychologists, A is no longer

A and B becomes Z. They only make things worse. They confuse the confused.'

We walked along slowly, birds winging their way freely through the blue sky. The closeness of her so strange, the familiarity of her touch so strange . . . and yet . . . so exciting.

'Have you seen many psychologists?'

Had I seen many psychologists? In the last two years or more I had seen so many that I'd lost count. In the last three weeks there'd been a different one every day. They'd all asked different questions, probing for answers. Not the answers I wanted to give . . . but the answers they wanted to hear . . . and they would run circles around me until they got the answer that mattered to their vision of the world. Everyone of them had been different. Brutal . . . nice . . . aggressive . . . mixed up . . . soft . . . hard . . . childish . . . superior. But not once had one of them been prepared to listen to me. Not one of them had understood what it was like to feel real pain . . . not the pain to the body . . . but the pain inside . . . the pain of not knowing who or what you were . . . of walking the streets and wondering whether one of the men walking along was your father . . . or building a dream of what your mother was like and then looking for her as the people shoved you to one side. Yes . . . I'd seen too many of them . . . and none of them could help me.

'Yes.'

'And?'

She wanted to know so much . . . and suddenly I knew she was listening . . . she wanted to listen. Could it be true.

'They always talked around me, through me, over me, but never to me personally. They always told me that all the trouble I was in was because of me. But it's not true. I didn't choose to be without parents. I didn't choose to live in that brutal foster home. I didn't start the fight in the school. I stole food because I was hungry. I didn't start the fight in the remand home . . . I only reacted to the situation which was arising. I didn't voluntarily go into the solitary confinement cell . . . I was dragged screaming into it. I didn't voluntarily ask to be beaten, I was held against the wall by two grown men and beaten until I was near unconscious. I didn't do all those things myself . . . they were done to me. But these psychologists . . . they kept excusing the adults . . . the people who did it . . . and tried to make me believe it was all my doing. All I ever wanted was to experience the love of that one woman who mattered so much to me . . . that woman of my dreams . . . my mother. I asked them who I was? From where I came, and where I was going . . . the lies they told ranged from . . . they're dead . . . to you never had a mother or father. Lies . . . lies and more lies . . . and more lies'.

I felt her arm tighten around my shoulder and hadn't realised my arm had encircled her waist. After that there was nothing but tears . . . and more tears and more tears. The dam had broken, years of hell came out, poured out. And I experienced something for the first time in my life . . . the other half of the world was soft, warm, comforting, and as strong as an ancient rock. It could bend, it could mould itself to smooth over the imperfections of my world until perfection was achieved. And suddenly I knew what love was all about.

3

She stopped the car on a hill and pointed across to a large, grey stoned, building that basked in the sun on the far side of the valley. It was an impressive sight. Big, square, three floors, massive windows. An old gentleman's house which had been added to over the years until it now fulfilled the function assigned to it. The drive leading up to it was more than a mile long and in it's day the house must have been impressive and belonging to an extremely wealthy family.

'That's your new home for a while. Sedbury Park.'

I watched as the massive stone building changed colour when a cloud passed between it and the sun.

'What's that river I can see in the distance, beyond the trees?'

'Oh, that. That's that River Severn. It completely borders one side of the estate on it's way to the sea. And in the next year or so, they'll begin the construction work on the Severn Bridge which will span the river.'

I didn't want the journey to come to an end. I had got an understanding with her that I didn't want to share with others. She must have known what was going through my mind, her hand stroked mine.

'How long will I be here?'

The smile slowly left her face.

'I'm not sure. It depends on a lot of things. You'll be studied, reports will be made, then they'll be studied and recommendations made. You'll certainly have to stay here for twelve months at least.'

'And what will you recommend?'

I liked to see her laugh, the cares of the world fell away

from me as well as her.

'I have very little to do with the decision-making, I'm what you could call a probationary officer here. I'm here only to learn, then I'll move on.'

The words hurt, considerably. And she saw it. She covered her mistake quickly.

'I'll be here for the next twelve months, so we'll see a lot of each other . . . if you want to.'

I looked across to the far building and wondered what it would be like there. It didn't seem so bad knowing she would be there as well . . . but something was telling me not to trust her . . . some devil inside me kept saying she would hurt me. Love can sometimes be blind and deaf in such inexperienced hands.

'I would like it.'

'Good.'

She really sounded like she meant it.

'We'd better get going or else we'll be too late for lunch. And you must certainly be hungry after that long trip.'

We'd stopped and eaten on the way, and anyway, how can anyone be hungry when they're about to be launched into a new life. I couldn't bring myself to answer as she started the engine, instead my heart began to hammer the walls of my chest.

I prayed for all sorts of things to happen as the vehicle gathered speed. I was scared to death of what I was about to be confronted with. I'd heard so many stories about these places. About how tough they were, and how brutal the inmates were. I'd heard about the jailers who liked to call themselves school masters beating people half to death . . . and I'd heard about the solitary confinement cells . . . and that's what really frightened me. In these places they were used frequently . . . for up to a week or ten days at a time.

We drove past the gatekeeper's lodge, the man eyed us suspiciously until he recognised the driver, and then he waved his hand cheerily. She drove very slowly up the long drive, but you couldn't stop the inevitable as we drove through the second set of gates, massive ornate gates that had at one time stood sentry to the horse-drawn coaches which had passed through them. The massive pillars which surrounded the front door seemed to close in around us as we drove into the shaded porch.

I followed her through the ten foot high doors into an incredibly cool marbled hall of such massive proportions as to be big enough to hold at least two normal houses. Even the gleaming marble staircase which swept up one side of the hall was like something out of a film and under it was a massive open fireplace that must have at one time filled the great cavernous hall with warmth. I looked directly up to the roof which seemed to be miles away and could see faces looking down at me from the different balconies.

'Headmaster. This is Geoffrey Dunstan Dawson, the young man I brought down from Birmingham.'

I quickly turned my head to look at the man who called himself 'Headmaster' and was surprised to be looking at a man whose weathered face, roman nose and moustache gave him the air of a real country gentleman. I looked down at the hand which was held out to me, it was work worn, it was the hand of an honest man. When I shook it, it felt good.

'Hello, Geoffrey. How do you do? Did you have a good trip here? It's quite a long way for you.'

'Yes Sir. It was a good trip. I've never seen cows before.'

The man laughed, a good honest bass laugh from such a tall thin frame.

'Well, we have quite a few cows here which you can get a much closer look at. We have our own farm here, and we have a forest. What would you like to do? Work on the farm, in the forest, or learn a trade like bricklaying or something in that line?'

'I'd like to work in the forest, I like trees.'

He looked me up and down with a very critical and experienced eye.

'Hmumm. I think we might have to wait a little while until you've put on some weight. That's extremely hard work and requires a lot of strength. You look a bit underweight at the moment, I think you might have a little difficulty in using a woodman's axe! Do you know how much a woodman's axe weighs and how big it is?'

'Yes, sir. One third the man's height, and weighs between four and five pounds.'

The man stood slowly up to his full height and drew air through his nose noisily.

'Hmmm. Very good. Looks like we just might make a woodsman out of you.'

He turned to Ann Summers.

'I believe he's to go into Chepstow house. If you'll find the senior boy he can show him around the school and get him settled in.'

'Yes, sir. But if you have no objections I would like to do it.'

There was an audible pause as the two looked at each other, words weren't necessary. She had decided an exception to the rules should be made. He accepted it.

'Good idea, Miss Summers. Lunch is in half an hour.'

Half an hour. That was as long as he'd allow her to change the rules for me, then it would be back to the routine of the establishment.

It was the shortest half hour I'd ever known. And when she left me with the senior boy of Chepstow house, her handshake was prolonged, her eyes full of feeling. When she left the school a year later she took something of me with her.

The title senior "boy" was somewhat of an understatement. The tall well built 18-19-year-old with a face full of stubble, was no boy.

'My oh my. You're quite a dandy, aren't you?'

I looked down at my clothes and shoes, and had every right to be proud of them. They were exceptional.

'Got any cigarettes? Money? Sweets? Books or anything like that. If so, give them to me and I'll put it into safe keeping.'

I couldn't help smiling. I'd been warned about that trick almost on my first day inside the remand centre.

'What are you smiling at?'

'Sorry. Just something someone said to me a while ago.'

A while ago. My goodness, three weeks seemed like three years, so much had happened.

'No. I really don't have anything. Just empty pockets.'

I saw the annoyance cross his face. Now he started to search me. He patted each pocket, then shoved his fingers inside. When he'd finished and there was nothing there, he stepped back.

'How long are you in for?'

'Three years.'

'What did you do?'

'Stole food, and got into a fight.'

The eyebrows lifted.

'G.B.H. huh?'

Grievious Bodily Harm was something I don't think I'd been charged with, but one never knew. "Keep something in hand" was something I'd learnt in the last few weeks. Don't acknowledge anything, but don't deny it until you have to.

'You're a bit young for the rough stuff. How old are you?'

'Thirteen.'

He was impressed. But he was going to find out what my financial capacity was, whether it would be worth cultivating me with some debts, just to get me on his team.

'Have you told your parents to send you food parcels with cigarettes, and matches and food stuff, tooth paste, books, soap etc? Valuable stuff, good for trading.'

'No.'

'You'd better do it, quick. You can write them a letter today, I'll dictate it to you so they send the right stuff. Plenty of cigarettes and money. The cigarettes are put into the bank for you, and you can have an issue of two a day. Though you might be a bit young, but you could always 'give' yours to someone else . . . like a friend.'

He was implying he would be my friend . . . for a price.

'What's your father do for a living?'

'Dead.'

I saw his face change. He was calculating my financial worth with reduced credit levels.

'Mother.'

'Dead.'

I had hit rock bottom in the credit rating. He lost interest immediately and looked around for someone else to look after me. When he saw someone he whistled for him to come across.'

'Take care of him. Give him the works.'

Then he was gone. I looked up at the sullen face and saw another school bully standing in front of me. Fat . . . drawn down mouth . . . sullen look on the face . . . spiteful eyes. His hand slammed me back against the wall, as his eyes swivelled over the landscape to check that no one was in sight. His tongue flicked across his lips as he roughly searched me. Finally he stood back.

'Where is it?'

'What?'

'The stuff you brought with you?'

'I didn't have anything. The other one found that out when he searched me.'

He stepped forward and roughly pulled my jacket open, what he was looking for I don't know.

'What are you doing, Davis.'

The voice was sing-song, pleasant on the ear. But there was a menace to it which the untrained ear would certainly not have picked up. The boy turned around, nearly jumping out of his skin with fear as the man approached.

Suddenly Davis was writhing in agony, his mouth wide open.

'What is the matter now, Davis?'

Again that pleasant sing song voice which came from the five foot something high, and five foot something wide man who was stood in front of me . . . smiling.

'Sir . . . please, sir . . . you're stood on my . . . foot.'

The man acted so surprised, as if he wouldn't hurt a fly . . . and if he did . . . it would be with deep regret.

'Oh, I'm so sorry Davis. But you always seem to be getting under my feet just lately.'

He didn't make a move to relieve the pressure on Davis's foot. He just stood a little firmer on it. The boy began to sink to his knees, his mouth open in agony.

'Stay where you are, Davis.'

The boy stood up again.

'My name is Bevan. I'm the building master here. Bricks and mortar, and that stuff. How would you like to join my group? We'd have to fatten you up a bit, nothing a bit of hard work wouldn't cure.'

'I . . . err . . . I don't mind hard work . . . I thought I could go to forestry . . .'

'Where are you from?'

'Birmingham.'

'No forests there, boy. Birmingham needs bricklayers. Good. What house are you in?'

'Chepstow.'

His face split into beams of laughter.

'Good, my boy. That's my house. You'll be a 'bricky' before you leave this place. I'll have you laying bricks on nothing but fresh air.'

As he turned, the bulk of his weight ground down on the toes of the boy who seemed to shrink with the pain.

'Take care of him. He belongs to my department. I want him delivered there this afternoon . . . without any damage.'

Suddenly the square Welshman grabbed the large envelope I'd been carrying all the time.

'Give me that thing before it melts in your hot paw.'

He opened the package and then extracted the life that lay inside it. It was mine, and belonged to me.

'I'll see you at three o'clock this afternoon, don't be late.'

Then he was gone. Even though he'd spoken in a rough and direct manner, it hadn't worried me. Few people in my life had wasted any pleasantries on me. From then on and for the next few hours I had to report to every department in the school, which included things as diverse as basket making, joinery, metal work, science, plumbing, painting, mechanical engineering and electrics. Apart from the farm, the forest and the kitchens, I'd seen everything. Except for one small item which I will relate in it's entirety.

As we'd just come out of the new toilets block, built by Mr Bevan's department; we walked past some very old but solidly built stables which at one time had been the tack rooms for the old house. I saw the boy who'd been showing me around surreptitiuosly make his way across the rough ground until he was stood at the middle of three doors, and then he began to search the ground intensely. My curiosity got the best of me.

'What are you looking for?'

'Stay still and be quiet. Watch out there's no one coming and I'll tell you in a minute.'

I quickly looked around me, but there was no one in sight. At least, I couldn't see them. What I never found out until later, was the fact that where we were stood now was a veritable hunting ground, and it was watched night and day. Suddenly I heard the curse and turned around. Whatever he'd been looking for, he hadn't found it. Then he beckoned me across.

'This place here is sacrosanct. In here works a man called Bill Eeney. He's the maintenance man here. Whenever anything breaks down, you call Bill Eeney.'

'What's so special about him?'

'His Tobacco!'

'What?'

'His tobacco! He smokes St Julian Tobacco, hand made cigarettes. He drops his cigarette ends here and there. They are the finest currency in the entire place. If you could get together a tin full of his cigarette ends, you could buy anything you want in this place. Even an escape route.'

I looked around me, we were in the open air.

'Who needs an escape route, there aren't any locked doors or bars here?'

The look he gave me told me I had a lot to learn.

'You're miles from anywhere here. You have to travel at least twenty miles in any direction before you can even get a train . . . if you have the money. A tin full of his tobacco could get you a road map, clothes, directions and food.'

'How?'

I was so ignorant, yet this really intrigued me.

'By bartering. We have a sort of committee here that looks after escapees. If you can pay the price they want, then they'll furnish you with all the information you need to get away. And a tin of Bill Eeney's tobacco is your passport to freedom.'

'Won't any tobacco do?'

The shake of his head was emphatic.

'No! Bill Eeney's or nothing. And there are 200 other boys trying to find the same thing.'

'Does he work alone?'

'No, if you can become a stoker in the boiler room, then you have the best chance of working as Bill Eeney's helper. As his helper you are allowed in his workshop, and able to empty his rubbish boxes. That's where he throws most of his cigarette ends.'

'How long can you stay on that job?'

'Three months. Unlimited freedom and privileges. Exactly the correct length of time to fill a half ounce tim of Bill Eeney's.'

'How do you get the job if everyone in the place is after his cigarette ends. You don't stand a chance in hell of finding enough ends to get the job.'

'This job you can't buy. Bill Eeney picks you for the job himself. You have to be good at many things and have a sense of humour like him. He's got a sense of humour as brittle as a dry stick. If he picks you to work as his assistant, then you've made it. There's no more cleaning jobs, washing up, scrubbing floors, cleaning boots or anything. You get extra food, start early in the mornings and finish late at night, go into town with him, but most important of all, you get every one of his cigarette ends whilst you're with him. Five Bill Eeneys and you can live comfortable for a week. Twenty Bill Eeneys and you'll have an army of slaves. A tin full . . . you are the richest man in the place . . . providing no one finds out about it. Then you could end up in some drain, with broken bones and your tobacco gone. Wherever Bill Eeney goes . . . there are at least fifty pairs of eyes following him, waiting for him to drop his long cigarette ends on the ground. Then it's every man for himself.'

I felt a thrill of excitement course through my veins. This was living on the edge of the knife. The rules were very clear and unambiguous. There was a man, and his tobacco. And his tobacco was the key to anything which was humanly possible in this place. You knew that every single member of this place had the same objective in mind, so it was the survival of the smartest and the strongest and no holds barred. Even the world outside wasn't that exciting. Suddenly I had the feeling I was where I belonged.

From there on for the rest of the school tour, it was only an anti-climax. True there were other possibilities to make capital for bartering, but there was nothing which had the equivalent purchasing power of a Bill Eeney dog end.

When I met the matron, the wife of the headmaster, I met a woman who was a very haughty version of her husband. When she talked to you, it was from the towering height of six feet four inches. One inch of that was attained by her permanently tilted back head which she got from looking down her nose at the dregs of society.

'And who are you?'

'Dawson.'

The hawk eyes pinned me to the floor.

'Matron . . . you address me as Matron. Is that clear?'

'Yes, Matron.'

She lifted what I now recognised as my file, and studied the top sheet and read it out allowed.

'Three years. Without chance of remission. Charges not

specified. Refer to central files, Birmingham City Council.'

Again the eyes.

'What did you do?'

'I stole some food. Got into a fight, injured somebody.'

'Ahhhhh. A G.B.H..'

She said it almost as if tasting the flavour of a challenge to her authority.

'So, you like it rough do you? Well you can have it rough if you want. In this place we'll break your urge to damage others.'

She was tall, black haired, with dark eyes, and had a certain slender strength that was about as feminine as a ring tailed Cobra. And for a thirteen year old boy, she was terrifying. The rest of the staff in the clothes room were small, fat and round homely type of women who spent most of their time laughing. They soon ran to fulfil the orders of the Matron so that she could sign my issue papers and leave as quickly as possible. When she had gone, everybody breathed a sigh of relief and the atmosphere relaxed considerably.

I hated the idea of separating with the clothes I had come down from Birmingham with, but I had no other choice. They were traded in for a pair of khaki military type shorts, military type shirt of the same colour, grey socks, a pair of boots which were worn for the whole day and a pair of shoes for the evening and weekends. When I had a shower before changing, it was in a very long shower room that could accommodate more than eighty at a time. Somehow I didn't like the idea of standing alone in this huge building waiting for the water to come down the mile long pipe.

The hours ran into days and the days ran into weeks. I adjusted to the routine better than I had thought possible. The brutality that I had become used to elsewhere, didin't exist here in the same form. There were very few unwritten rules in the establishment, and they were easy to follow:

1. Don't ever run to a master and grass on an inmate. Penalty: severe beating in the toilets if found out.

2. Don't steal from your fellow inmates. Penalty: severe beating in toilets.

3. If you are escaping, then consult the escape committee who can, if necessary, protect those around you from suspicion. Penalty: cold shouldered and loss of unwritten

privileges. Plus beating in bed.

4. Anyone who is responsible for an inmate receiving 'extra time' is best advised to escape immediately and hope to be transferred to another establishment.

5. No one is permitted to criticise or make bad remarks about an inmates close family, or read another's mail. Penalty: All of the above.

6. Anyone who accumulates any quantity of Bill Eeneys and allows it to become public knowledge stands to lose the haul by any means possible. No redress.

7. It is the duty of all inmates to prevent the staff from finding out anything detrimental to the inmates. There is but one standard answer to all questions. 'Don't know'. Penalty: a good hiding or heavy fine imposed by the senior boys.

Those were the basic rules laid down by the inmates, for a peaceful life. But of course, the inevitable fight broke out every single hour of the day. The commonest cause, encroachment into another inmate's very private area — i.e. getting too near when he needs time alone. Asking too many questions and the most serious of all, being too long in the area of his private locker. They were very basic and understandable rules, and easily followed. There were other rules also, but these were the social rules that were never spoken about or even referred to, but never the less enforceable with a fast and unexplained smack in the ear.

There was also the inevitable private vendetta, and threats of violence flying through the air and cowardice was severely frowned upon, but all in all it was a better society than I had experienced on the outside.

Each day we were forced to drink a cup of cocoa which had a strange taste to it. When I questioned further, I was informed that there was bromine in the cocoa. The bromine was to suppress any sexual urges the boys had. But after some of the things I'd witnessed I wondered whether they'd been using the correct dosage.

It was a few weeks after being there that I met one of the true characters of the place. He was nicknamed 'Ginger' because of the colour of his hair. And he was famous for his inventive mind. Ginger had been sent down for eighteen months for being in possession of material for breaking and entering.

Now, Ginger was no criminal, he just liked inventing things and trying them out to see if they worked. Well, one day he'd invented something which he said could bypass even the most sophisticated of alarm systems, but the problem was that no one would allow him to try it out. So he'd gone down to the local bank, and lo and behold it had functioned and he'd opened the back door of the bank without a sound being heard.

Ginger had one big fault. Without his glasses he was as blind as a bat. On the day of his big coup on the bank door, he dropped his glasses, and was found by a policeman on his rounds groping around on the floor looking for his glasses with the back door of the bank wide open. Needless to say, nobody believed him, the magistrate the least.

Ginger had served two years of his eighteen months because he was always getting into trouble trying out his inventions. The latest event had been something which had grabbed the interest of all car thieves in the school, of which there were quite a few.

He had invented some contraption which he swore could bypass the ignition system of a vehicle and enable the vehicle to be stolen with the least amount of effort. The problem? There were no vehicles available for him to try out the device. Well, not exactly true, there were the cars from the masters but it was considered too dangerous to try it out on one of them because of the risk something could go wrong. So it had been decided he should wait for one of the delivery vehicles to come to the school for him to be able put his device to the test.

Ginger was a really nice fellow, with the typically distracted mind of the true scientist, which sometimes made him forget important details. He was also impatient to try out his inventions, before the boys were properly set up for the 'test'. This ignition jumping kit was one of those occasions when Ginger was ahead of the crowd. He'd had to wait three days for a vehicle to come to the school, and then it turned out to be the refuse collection truck rather than the baker's van which had been expected. But Ginger was not to be deterred, if the refuse truck was the only vehicle available, then the refuse truck it had to be.

The rest of us were hidden in the toilets spying from the

windows, whilst Ginger advanced on the truck the contraption
in his hand. We watched as he climbed up into the vehicle
and sat in the driver's seat. Then we saw his thick bottle
glasses grinning up at us as he did something under the
steering wheel. Suddenly the trucks engine sprung into life and
the vehicle began to move in violent jerks . . . backwards. We
could all see the look of consternation on Ginger's face, his
tongue stuck out the corner of his mouth, looking straight
ahead as if he couldn't understand why the vehicle kept going
in the wrong direction.

'Jesus . . . he can't drive', was the chorus that echoed
around the toilet as the heavy vehicle kept going backwards
and crashed into the dustbins, demolished the clothes room
window, finally coming to rest firmly on top of the boiler room
steps, trapping the one and only Bill Eeney in the boiler room,
whose voice could be heard roundly cursing the driver of the
truck.

Those who weren't supposed to be in the area ran off to
howls of laughter as Ginger hared across the ground, wires
trailing wildly from his pocket. To those who could justify
being in the area, myself included, because I was on toilet
cleaning detail, it was a sight to watch the dustmen trying to
squeeze past the truck screaming at each other, whilst Bill
Eeney urged them on with language we'd never heard from
him before.

It was as the summer of the first year in Chepstow was
pulling to an end, and after I had spent many an hour on my
own watching the waters of the River Severn running past me
on their journey out to sea and thinking about what was
eating away at me, when I finally came to a decision.

Somehow or other I had to find out who I was and where I
came from. I had been watching for weeks the rest of the
inmates receiving visits from their families. I had watched the
happiness, I had watched the tears, I had watched the
emotions, the arguments, the bond between sons and mothers,
brothers and sisters. And I had watched the confidence these
bonds created in my friends and enemies alike. I could see how
for one or two weeks after the visits the tensions within the
place were at their lowest ebb, with everyone too busy
discussing their families and their hopes and dreams, until,
towards the last week before the new visits when one walked

carefully, even around ones own best friends. For a while, everyone had the feeling they belonged somewhere ... to someone.

Whilst watching all this, I hadn't realised that a hole was growing inside me. A hole so big, there was no way to fill it.

I had become irritable, and difficult to talk to. Also, I found I was reluctant to become involved in the machinations of the inmates in their constant battle against their jailers. And even the most trivial of things seemed to irritate me. Friends no longer tried to involve me in things, leaving me to wander through the daily routine blindly without realising what I was doing.

I would sit in trepidation of someone calling out my name at mail time, fearing that someone somewhere knew that I existed. But it never happened, that fear never came to reality, because only my jailers knew that I existed.

Then one day, during another of these weekend visits, I found I could no longer bare to watch the kaleidoscope of emotions unfolding before me. I yearned for someone to come from that outside world and say that for them ... I was ... and am. The loneliness was destroying me ... slowly ... the loneliness of the unwanted.

I had staggered away to be alone with my misery, tears burning their way through my skin until they shrivelled the tissue of my heart. I was alone, and would remain so for the rest of my life.

Even to this very day, as I write this book, I know there is something inside me which is missing. Something which other people take for granted; that feeling of belonging. That feeling of knowing who you are and where you come from. That feeling of completeness as a person ... that feeling which only the most special of persons can give you. That love which is given unconditionally, given freely and not expected to be returned but gratefully accepted when it is. It has existed ... fleetingly ... only to be dashed when I haven't fulfilled the expectations of those who have demanded more than I have up to now learnt to give. That turned away head, the apologies, the avoidance, the blank looks, the angry words, the insults, the impatience, the unanswered telephone, the hours of hope followed by the hours of loneliness, all those things which make the hole grow bigger when you are begging for time to close it. When I reach out my hand . . . who's there to take it?

So I had wandered away, walking unconsciously to a place where I felt at least part of the world about me. I had walked across the fields which belonged to the farm, stopping only when I reached the high bank which the river had cut during the centuries. There I had sat, hour after hour, alone with myself. Until finally the decision was reached.

There was only one thing I could do. I would start a campaign to try and find my parents. I would start questioning, and questioning. Demanding answers to questions which up to now had only been answered with lies. Lies which made others comfortable with their consciences, but myself lost and desperate. Having come to my decision, I felt better, much better.

I sat there a little longer watching the sun go down, without even realising I was doing it. Then suddenly I realised where I was and what I was doing. It was getting dark, which meant it was already past the last roll call by at least two hours. I was missing, presumed escapee.

There was no way I could get out of it, no matter what I said, there was going to be trouble. My mind raced over the possibilities of just walking away into the night, following the rippling waters below me until I stopped wandering. But I knew deep down inside of me I would have to abandon that idea if I wanted answers to my questions. If I escaped, even the privilege of talking to the Governor would be withdrawn, and he was the only man who had the power to help me in my quest.

I secretly said goodbye to the river, knowing full well I would never be able to come back again, then set off at full run across the ploughed fields towards the dark buildings.

It was my luck that this night, the duty officer would be a tall, thin, cadaverous, ex air force officer who took his duties very seriously. He'd been on duty for the last roll call, and had carried out the customary search of the buildings for me. When no one had found me, he'd immediately reported me as an escapee and informed the Police.

He saw me approaching the back door of the building and assumed correctly that I was hoping to get inside without anyone seeing me.

I managed to get the door open without causing any noise

and had just got inside when I was propelled with some force into the wall and my arm was twisted savagely up my back.

'So, Dawson! Thought you were going to sneak in without anyone knowing, or perhaps you were hoping to break into the kitchen to steal some food to make good your escape.'

'No, sir . . . I swear . . . I was out near the forest . . . and just forgot . . .'

'Tell that to your mother, she'll believe anything. You are a reported escapee. What were you after? Money? Or was it food?'

My arm was given a violent jerk and it felt as if it would snap at the socket. My face was squashed into the wall and his knee was pressing the centre of my back. There was hardly any way to answer him. He grabbed a handful of my hair, and with my arm still up my back, he marched me purposely towards the Governor's office.

It took a phone call to the Governor's private quarters and a three minute wait before the man opened the door of the office. I knew what was going to come, and felt the fear well up inside me. Solitary confinement was the last thing I wanted now.

'So, Mr Roach. What's the problem? Ahhh! Dawson! Well well. To be honest young man . . . you were the last person I expected to try an escape. What happened? Did you suddenly lose your courage? Or did you lose your way? Escaping is not so easy as it sounds. Huh.'

'Sir . . . I didn't try to escape . . . I was sat on the riverbank watching the water, and forgot the time.'

The serious brown eyes watched me over the beak nose, they narrowed, studied and finally came to a decision after looking at the mud on my shoes.

'Mr Roach . . . your opinion.'

'I've been watching him for some time, sir. And have seen his peculiar behaviour. Sticking on his own, not having anything to do with the others . . . always thinking . . . silent. He must have been planning this for weeks . . . only when he got away did he realise how difficult it was and gave up. He tried to sneak into the back door. Either he was going to break into the offices for money . . . or else he was going for the kitchens and some extra food. Luckily we know this trick from other escapees . . . so I was waiting for him at the back door.'

It seemed to take an eternity for the Governor to make his mind up. And when he did my heart fell to the floor.

'Well done, Mr Roach.'

He looked at me, and I could see he was in no mood to listen to what I had to say.

'You've disappointed me, Dawson. Your record in this twelfth year of your life is abysmal. In fact, it's my impression you are anti-authoritarian. I think you've got a chip on your shoulder which needs knocking off. And I'm going to do it. In this place you're going to learn to live with the rest of the people who are here, and can accept that they've got to serve out their sentences. This will be recorded on your file.'

Then he turned around and selected a cane from his rack. It was the switch cane. Split into four pieces at the end and bound with sticking tape to add weight. He made a test strike on the desk and the crack cannoned off the walls.

'Twelve strokes, six on the hands, six on the backside. Three days solitary confinement. No exercise period . . . He's already had enough tonight. Diet . . . Bread and water. Hold your hands out!'

I knew this was going to be painful and the only sound I could hear was my heart hammering against the walls of my chest. Two hands together, held out in front of me, jerking as they anticipated the blow. Sweat coated my skin, and when it came, I could feel the blood rush into my mouth as my teeth clamped down on the tongue.

'Keep still!'

I could see by the redness of the Governor's face, he was annoyed. An inmate was supposed to take his punishment . . . like a man.

'Count them out, Mr Roach.'

'One . . .'

'Two . . .'

'Three.'

'Keep still, boy. That one doesn't count. Mr Roach.'

The split cane crashed down again on the edges of the fingers driving all feeling from them. I though I was about to lose them.

'Three . . .'

'Four . . .'

Pain cannoned around inside my body at an enormous rate,

I tried to live up to the school's tradition of taking the punishment in silence, but sounds escaped through my gritted teeth as I tried to take the blows. I had difficulty in holding the fingers out straight anymore.

'Five . . .'

Eternity seemed to pass between me and the cane. Pain swimmed around in the head, making it difficult to know what was happening. I could taste the salt from the sweat and tears and the bitter sweat taste of the blood on my lips.

'Six! Bend over the desk . . . shirt out of the trousers. Move!'

I tried . . . I really tried . . . but how can you tell someone you're in pain . . . how can you tell them you can't use your hands. The matter was taken out of my hands as someone roughly dragged me to the desk and bent me forcibly over it.

'Mr Roach . . . The count!

I straightened up with the first blow, even though Mr Roach had the weight of his body on top of me. He fought me back down to the desk . . . but with difficulty.

'No . . . No . . . No more!'

The words came out in a croak, the blood sticking in my throat, threatening to choke me.

'One . . .'

Stars, coloured spots, rainbow colours, dashed across my tightly squeezed eyes. The desk moved with my struggles and both men came after me. Anger and shouts boomed across the office.

'Hold him still, Roach. He's not going to get away. Start the count again!'

'One . . .'

'Two . . .'

The voice echoed and boomed across my brain, darkness dulling the words. Red filled my eyes and somehow I seemed to be floating above myself looking dispassionately down.

'Three . . .'

'Four . . .'

The pain was a faraway ache, just like the voices. My body twitched but I was no longer part of it.

'Five . . .'

'Six . . .'

I knew nothing about the journey to the solitary confinement cell. Just as I knew nothing about the first two days in it. I only seemed to come to on the third day, when the matron came in and bathed the wounds on my hands and backside. She said nothing to me, but I could tell by her silence she was annoyed . . . but at who? By the time I was let out that night, I was able to walk again. And as I walked the long corridors back to my dormitory, I could feel the eyes of the world watching every step. Nothing was said to me for a few days . . . each and every one of the inmates seemed to be subdued . . . as if they had personaly felt the pain I had suffered.

It took a long time for the truth to come out, and was only told to me by a boy who was leaving the place. The whole school had heard the beating, the halls and corridors acting like loudspeakers. They had heard the strokes, and had heard the screams, and had heard the count. Fifteen strokes from the switch cane. More than had ever been given in punishment in the time that most of the boys had been there. It was said that the Governor had got drunk afterwards when he could no longer stand the sounds of the screams from the solitary cell, whilst the Matron had tried to repair the damage. He was not seen again for more than a week. Mr Roach left the school a month later.

It was not an intentional act, but I found myself staying even more away from everyone. They never ever said anything to me, and I suspect they knew better what was wrong than all the experts at the school. I needed a very long time to bring myself to the point where I could accept the word of the jailers. They spoke to me, but what they said didn't register. I was in a far away place, a place where the brutality of the world couldn't get at me. Where the sun shone all the time, and I could walk over the horizon into the arms of someone who wanted me. Whenever I tried to look at her face, it was always hazy so I would never be able to recognise who it was. But her happiness and love filled that huge hole inside me.

I suppose, considering the way I had been behaving, it was inevitable someone came up with the idea that I was crazy. I know it must have been debated for some time at the monthly staff meetings, because one day I was called into the Governor's office. When I stood in front of him, I could see he was not the same man I had met a year before. He had aged, and his burden was etched in creases on his face.

'Good morning, Dawson.'

'Good morning, sir.'

'Tell me. Are you unhappy here?'

'No, sir.'

He seemed to take a long time to think about the answer.

'I think it's time you told someone about your problems.'

'I don't have any problems, sir.'

Again he seemed to take a long time over the answer.

'I'm sorry. But I don't agree with you. Your attitude is beginning to cause problems here. You are disturbing the harmony of this place. Some of the boys are openly frightened of you, and my staff say there's no way to talk to you or to get you to join in anything. It's no good, Dawson. My staff are asking for your transferral to another establishment.'

'Who am I, sir. And where are my parents?'

I could see he was holding himself in check, but his answer was loud enough.

'Dawson! I'm tired of this theme. You've been told a dozen times, your parents are dead. And you are an orphan. Your mother died when you were born and your father a short while later. You have no parents anymore. Why don't you get that into your head?'

He looked at the paper that was in front of him, as if he was making a painful decision. Then he picked up a pen and signed his signature on the bottom.

'Tomorrow morning I want you to collect your clothes from Matron and be ready to go to Bristol. In the meantime you'll go across to see Miss Summers.'

I sat in front of her, without a desk between us. She looked at me, and the old feelings for her welled up inside me. Soft, gentle, steady as a rock. When she looked at me, I could feel the warmth of her wrapping itself around me.

'You've changed a lot, Geoff. You're very much grown up. How old are you now?'

'Nearly fourteen.'

She seemed to study me for a while, and then sighed.

'Time goes quickly . . . Do you know why you've been sent to me?'

'No.'

'Truly?'

'I was just told to report to you.'

She nodded her head, as if she had expected the answer.

'Do you trust me, Geoff?'

'I always have.'

'Enough to go to a hospital with me, tomorrow?'

Warning bells were going off in my head.

'What sort of hospital?'

'A mental hospital.'

My head was filling with every possibility, and a million questions. But only one came to mind.

'Why?'

She took a long time to answer the question.

'For the last few months, in fact, at every staff meeting, you've become the focal point of the discussions. The masters have been making some strong complaints against you. One of them thinks you're dangerous . . . a time bomb waiting to go off . . . to use his words. One says you flare up into a temper at the slightest provocation, and when you fight it's as if your life is at stake. Another says you're gaining too much respect from the rest of the boys, bordering on fear. Another one thinks that your capacity to think in unconventional ways is frightening. Another says you spend too much on your own, more than what's good for you. In fact, to the point where you represent an unbalancing and disruptive influence on the team spirit of the other boys. The same man feels you may well become dangerous if you're pushed too hard and has even requested your transferral to a closed school or even a borstal.'

Borstals were surrounded by iron bars, locked doors, and very high walls. Which was good enough reason to justify the shudder that went down my back.

'Which brings me to tomorrow. I'm taking you up to Bristol to see one or two doctors who want to carry out some tests on you. They want to find out what makes you tick. We need to find out how you think and what you like and dislike, then perhaps we can find out what is best for you. You see, we only want to see you finally happy.'

The decision had been made a long time ago. But what would happen if I said, No! It didn't need thinking about. They had passed the job on to her because of our special relationship, they would crucify her.

'All right . . . Ann. I'll go with you.'

Using her name after all this time sent a wave of special feelings rushing through me. I could see also that it meant something to her.

'Thank you, Geoff, It makes things a lot easier. You see, this is my last job at the school. I leave at the end of the week. I asked for permission to delay my departure by two weeks, because I wanted to be there with you, when they do the tests.'

They roared into me at breakneck speed, all the fears I'd ever had. Although I'd been there, I'd had little chance to talk to her all the time I'd been there, I'd seen her about the school. It had been enough . . . she'd always been there. That special smile, even when she'd been in the company of one of the wardens. She'd become my life line . . . and I hadn't even realised it. I loved her. And now she was to leave . . . to leave my life a shattered ruin . . . afraid to even talk to someone in case they disappeared the following day. I felt as if I could have fallen into tiny pieces on the floor, such was the destructive value of her words. I fought hard to hold back the tears, but it was no good, they came out in huge great runs, my body wracked with sobs. Oh God, would it never stop! She came to me, and I held tight. How I needed her rock like calmness in a world which seemed to be falling apart.

I got into trouble before I was fifty yards from her office. One of the older boys (old enough to be in an adult prison) had been eyeing her office the whole time, and obviously had some idea in his head about his relationship to Ann Summers. He decided to air his views with me. It was all I needed, she meant too much to me to allow such things to be said. It took two very brawny warders to separate the two of us, with the boy bearing some nasty wounds. Only intervention by Ann Summers saved me from some heavy trouble, but one of the warders had the final word as he pointed a thick finger at me.

'Dawson. You're not long for this place. That I promise you. Even if I have to go to the governing board, I'll have you out of here before the month is out.'

And I knew he would do it. He was the Deputy Governor, and slated to take over in the next few months. My fate was sealed. Another roof, another bed. New faces, the same old problems and a hole which kept growing inside me.

4

The sun was just coming up over the horizon as she drove her car out through the gates. She'd got the duty warden to get me out of bed early, an early breakfast and we were on our way before the rest of the school had woken up.

'I hope you didn't mind leaving so early?'

I wanted to touch her, but I wasn't sure whether I should.

'No. I couldn't sleep anyway.'

'I'm sorry about yesterday. Did you get hurt?'

I looked at my grazed knuckles and felt the bruise under my eye. No I wasn't hurt . . . physically, 'No'.

'I've never had someone defend my honour before.'

'He said things which I didn't like.'

She seemed to be lost in thought for a minute.

'Yes. I know. I've had a lot of trouble with him. It's not easy to work in a place like this with young men like him.'

Her hand covered mine and then lifted it to her lips.

Bolts of fire shot through me.

"Thank you, I appreciate what you did.'

She drove on for a while, both of us lost in our own thoughts.

'I told the Governor I wanted to visit someone on the way to Bristol. It wasn't true, I just thought we could have a little more time together.'

She pulled her handbag onto her lap and fumbled through it until she found what she wanted. Then handed me a small parcel.

'I want you to have this. It's a present. You can open it now.'

With shaking fingers I tore the paper off to reveal a long

black box. When I opened it, there lay a watch on a bed of blue velvet. Words were impossible to find.

'Turn it over.'

On the back were inscribed the words.

'To Geoff. With all my love. Ann'

I gripped the watch until I could feel the skin of my knuckles go tight. It was the first thing which had ever been given to me. And that it should be from her meant more to me than I could find words to express. When I put the watch onto my wrist, it was never to be removed until the heat and moisture of the jungles of Borneo rotted the wrist band and it was lost forever. Forgive me, Ann. I would not have lost that watch for all the world.

The journey to Bristol seemed to take barely five minutes, but is was in fact a few hours, with stops here and there for sightseeing and coffee in a cafe. When we reached the imposing building which was our destination, I stood outside the car looking at the tall brick building that would have done better service as a prison . . . She pressed the doorbell, a key was turned in a lock and we were admitted. Ann could feel my back stiffen and my steps slow. she turned to look at me, her eyes pleading.

'Please. Trust me. I'll be with you all the time. Nothing is going to happen.'

Oh, how I wanted to trust her. But there were so many memories of locked doors, barred windows, and solitary confinement cells. Her outstretched hand begged me to trust her, and against all my instincts . . . I did.

We were led down long corridors by a stern faced woman in a white coat, past doors where the sound of screaming and hysterical laughter kept assaulting our ears. Finally we stopped at a steel door which was opened with a bunch of keys our guide produced.

The room had no windows, and the door was nothing better than a steel prison cell door. Even Ann was surprised and turned to question the guide.

'Are you sure you've got the right room?'

The woman looked at her, and then at me contemptuously.

'His name is Dawson? Sedbury Park, Approved School?'

'Yes . . . but this . . . it's nothing more . . .'

'The report says he's dangerous. We've got enough of his

kind here already. This is the correct room. Now if you'll just leave him, he'll be quite all right. The doctors will see him when they're ready and you can be sure he won't escape from here.'

I spun around on Ann, but she was already facing down the woman.

'I'm not leaving. You can lock the door. But I'll be inside.'

The woman was shocked.

'Miss Summers! I can't do that. It's not allowed. The prisoner is to be put into a cell . . . alone.'

Ann Summers walked into the cell and sat down on the bed.'You can tell the doctor I'm here with the 'Prisoner'. If he has to go into the cell . . . then I go with him.'

I was getting jabs of panic going through me, the walls of the room were beginning to close in.

The floor kept coming up to meet the ceiling as the woman's voice kept fading in and out. She became a monster barring my way out. She was closing the coffin down before I'd even died. Sweat broke out over my whole body as I began to fight for air.

I tried to stagger towards the door, but my legs didn't seem to want to take me and the door seemed to get further away. I hardly heard the heated exchange which took place because I was being literally dragged out by the arm. Ann was trying to stop my brain from bursting. She talked and talked, telling me to take deep breaths by a open window. Our guide was backing down the corridor under a barrage of abuse that would have done justice to a dockworker . . . from a doctor of all persons. I was helped into a large room with big windows and bars. It was filled with electronic machinery arranged around a hard bed stood in the middle of the room.

When I was lain on the bed, she went to the corner of the room and had a long conversation with the doctor. It seemed that she was well known here. And then I fell asleep.

I woke up to find Ann sitting next to me and someone behind me cutting my hair. She held her hand on my arm to tell me to stay still. The woman behind me carried on cutting my hair. Ann finally held a mirror for me to see what had been done, and I could see the hurt in her eyes. My hair had been butchered until there was tufts of it sticking up here and there, the rest looked like I'd been in an operating theatre.

Then the machines were wheeled closer to the bed and multi coloured suckers were attached to my head.

'You knew, didn't you Ann?'

She didn't answer, but held my hand tight.

"Why . . . Ann . . .Why couldn't you tell me the truth?'

It was twenty minutes or more before the doctors arrived, and when they did, it was like an army marching into the room. At the head of them was very pompous man who considered the rest of the world beneath his dignity. He marched to the bed and looked down at me.

'Well, Miss Summers. It's a very long time since we've seen you. I hear you're leaving your establishment. Where are you going?'

'Home. To look after my mother. At least she's normal, compared to some of the people I work with.'

I could feel the emnity between Ann and this man, and hoped it wouldn't get in the way of this examination. The man kept turning my head from side to side as if he was admiring some garden plant.

'Good. The file, Miss Summers. Do you have anything to add?'

Finally she stood up and faced the man.

'Nothing that would be called professionaly biased. It's called woman's intuition.'

I watched the man look over the top of his glasses at her, there was surprise in his eyes.

'I think we might get on better if you leave.'

'Sorry, professor. He's in my care. I take my duties seriously. I'm staying.

The man grunted and then turned away with the file in his hands. His disciples gathered around him like a protective wall as their master spoke. He was a man whom even I wouldn't have trusted to make a decision when to cross the road. Then he turned back to me and became business like.

'All right, young man. I want you to take your shoes off, belt off, empty your pockets, watch off, and tie. And be careful you don't disturb those wires on your head.'

When I had complied with his order, I gave the watch to Ann who was still sat next to me.

'All right, young man. The purpose of this exercise is to establish just what's wrong with you. Miss Summers has almost certainly explained why you're here, so I don't need to go into that. We're going to ask you a number of questions, which you will answer. On the machines around you will be recorded the amount of energy your brain requires to produce the answer, and which part of the brain is working. I want you to lie perfectly still, if you can't we can always tie you down. Do you want that?'

'No.'

The mans wintery smile beamed down on me, he seemed almost disappointed.

'Good. Then let's start.'

'Name.'

'Geoffrey Dawson.'

'Age?'

'Nearly fourteen.'

'How tall are you?'

'Ummm . . . not sure'

'Good. Are you left or right handed?'

'Right handed'

'Where were you born?'

'Birmingham.'

'How old are you?'

'You've already asked me that'

'Answer the question!'

'Nearly fourteen.'

'What school are you at?'

'Sedbury Park.'

'Do you like it there?'

'It's a prison.'

'Mark that one. Answer the question. Do you like it there?'

'No. It's a prison.'

'Where were you born?'

'Birmingham.'

I suddenly realised something was happening as I lay there. My body felt as though it was getting heavier and heavier, and my brain was beginning to fill my whole head. I was looking at a spot on the ceiling with such clarity that I found it hard to believe I was even taking part in the whole proceedings. Excitement began to well up inside me. I had found the key to these people.

'Where in Birmingham were you born?'

I suddenly needed no effort to answer the questions.

'Don't know.'

'What's your mother's name?'

'Don't know.'

'Father's name?'

'Don't know.'

There was a pause while some papers were ruffled. Then some of the doctors monitoring the machines got together.

'Are you sure the wires are connected properly?'

Someone rocked my head from side to side.

'Yes. Everything looks fine.'

'Young man. We don't seem to be getting the signals properly. I would like you to think harder about the questions. Take your time if you wish, but think harder.'

I dared not smile, they would most probably have known what I was thinking. They were trying to empty my head. Now I knew which direction I would be going.

'We're going to try again. Do you like the place you're at?'

'It's a prison.'

'Answer the damned question!'

I had absolutely no interest in answering the question. In my head it was crystal clear, nobody would be happy in a prison.

'You're not helping us, Dawson.'

'What's your favourite food?'

'Don't know.'

'Milk, Tea, what do you like best?'

'Don't know. Don't get enough to be able to choose.'

'What sport do you like best?'

'Rugby.'

'What do you want to do when you grow up?'

'Become a soldier.'

'Any particular unit?'

'Royal Marines.'

The chair scraped nearer.

'And what will you do?'

'Become a Commando.'

'That's a very tough job. Only the best get there.'

'I think I'll make it.'

'Do you like fighting?'

'I do what I have to do. If I'm forced to fight, I fight.'

'Your file says you're dangerous. You injure other people. Do you like it?'

'If I'm forced to fight, I fight.'

'Bite on this.'

A piece of rubber was forced between my teeth and then I felt two rubber things attached to the side of my head. The shock nearly lifted my body from the bed, I bit down involuntarily on the rubber hardly able to get enough air into my mouth. Straps were thrown over my body and I could hear in the distance Ann shouting as she was being removed from the room. The jolt came again and I could feel my body straining against the straps. Sweat soaked my body.

'Do you like hurting other people?'

I grunted through the rubber piece in my mouth, trying to spit out. My head rocked from side to side, but someone decided to hold it still.

'Answer my question! Do you like hurting other people?'

The shock came again and my body became rigid as it fought against the restraints. Then I suddenly fell back to the bed, feeling disjointed, as if my body had fallen apart.

My lungs were screaming for air, but I couldn't get any past the rubber piece. Someone took it out of my mouth and I gasped air in huge gulps into my tortured lungs.

'Do you like hurting other people?'

The voice was sadistic, low and cruel. I could feel his hot breath against my ear. All I could do was to rock my head from side to side, I couldn't find my voice, and my jaws ached fiercely from biting the rubber.

'G-o-o-d.'

I heard the professor walk away from the bed, he was conferring with his disciples. My head and my vision was spinning and I could feel the bile rising in my throat, I wanted to be sick and I was far too hot: I didn't want to close my eyes because the world wouldn't keep still and the bile was already choking me.

'He-l-p.'

I thrashed around and suddenly felt strange hands breaking the straps and turning me onto my side, I was immediately sick. I kept retching till there was nothing left in my stomach . . . just pain. Through the haze of my spinning brain I could feel rather than see the professor standing next to me.

'You brought that on yourself, young man. I asked you to co-operate. Now rest, and then we'll come back in an hour and start again.'

I felt the crowd leave the room, then a familiar figure was beside me. I could feel tears running down on to my cheek as she stroked my face, but I couldn't do anything. I was even too weak to tell her it wasn't her fault, and that no matter whatever happened I would always love her. I wanted to die, but couldn't . . . death wouldn't do me that favour.

She sat the entire time next to me, carefully wiping my face with a wet cloth until I began to feel better, and my vision slowly cleared. The eyes were red rimmed and the cheeks scoured with tears; they had hurt her more than they'd hurt me. I would get over it, she wouldn't.

It was two hours before they came back, during which time I'd held her hand and gathered my strength from her.

This time the professor wasn't there. And the rest of his disciples seemed to have had the steam knocked out of them. They were extra careful with me, and took great care to explain everything they were doing.

'Geoffrey. We're going to test your reactions to different coloured lights and we'll test your reflexes and a few nerves. There'll be no more pain. We're sorry about what happened before . . . It shouldn't have happened. Trust us now . . . trust us and work with us.'

I saw the pleading look on his face as he looked at Ann . . . she didn't trust him. Slowly she got up and came and stood next to my head, her hand on my shoulder. Finally I nodded my head.

They tapped my knees, ran sharp objects over the soles of my feet, scratched the skin on my arms. Made me watch a mass of flashing lights above my head as they changed colour. Then they unplugged me and helped me get up. My legs were weak and my head began to spin again, but after a few steps I felt my strength return and my head stopped spinning.

Then they put me through the process of picking out my favourite shapes from a multitude of others. The doctor asked why I had picked those particular shapes.

'Because you expected me to pick out other ones.'

The man looked at me, and finally nodded his head in a defeated manner.

'I think we can close the tests. Miss Summers. The professor's report will be with you tomorrow. Special messenger.'

One of the nurses handed me a ski-ing cap to cover my head, but I didn't put it on. Why should I be ashamed of what others have done to me, they are the ones who should be ashamed for the world to see what they'd done.

The last real pain that affected me deeply, happened only twenty four hours after getting back from Bristol. When we had arrived back at the school, it was late afternoon, and Ann took me back to her private rooms to cut my hair until it was respectable. She knew only too well how cruel the other boys could be, especially if I went amongst them looking like I did.

My departure from her is something special and precious to me and will never be shared with anyone else.

But the following day I was handed an envelope by the Governor personally. I didn't open it immediately, instead I walked across the fields until I came to my favourite spot on the bank above the wide river. Then I carefully opened it and read. I can honestly recall every word of the letter, because it is etched inside me.

Dear Geoff.

Forgive me for writing to you like this. But for me I think it would be easier.

I cannot face you knowing how much you trusted me, and then seeing what barbaric acts were carried out against you at the hospital. I cannot ask your forgiveness for what happened, but I know you'll give it anyway, because that's the way you are.

By the time this letter reaches you, I'll have left the school and in doing it this way I know I'll hurt you again. But I can't help myself anymore.

Today I had very long talks with the Governor and he advised me to leave immediately. There was no possibility I could any longer maintain a professional distance between you and I and I hadn't realised it until the Governor pointed it out to me. The problem is that I've loved you ever since we first met. The times I fought for you, I thought it was on a professional basis. Now I know it wasn't. I've asked one favour from the Governor and he has granted it. He is going to send you to a very special school near Birmingham where you'll have the best training possible to enable you to fulfill your wish to join the Royal Marines. I want you to work really hard and achieve your wish, because that would make me immensely happy. I know it will be difficult for you to understand why I must leave you this way, but later on you will realise why.

I have left ten pounds on your school account and hope you'll use it well.

Even though I won't be there with you, I want you to know that you're not on your own anymore. Take care, Geoff. I hope you'll always remember me.

My love to you only.
Ann.

Through the tears I looked out across the river and knew that somewhere across there was someone who cared for me, someone who made me realise what it was to love and belong. And like everything that has ever happened in my life, they have had to leave. My tears ran as fast as the river below me, the pain coursing through my body, and I screamed to the heavens for her return. I shouted till I was hoarse and I called her name a thousand times. But it was all carried on the wind, to the far and the deaf horizons.

I was on my knees on the ground the letter damp from my tears, my heart feeling as if it had been torn apart, when I heard the gentle voice of the Governor.

'Ann told me you would be here. She asked that you be left alone for as long as possible to give you time to get over it. She has explained many things which none of us understood. I came alone to talk to you. Is this where you were on the night you were reported as missing?'

I hadn't even realised it had got dark, night and day didn't matter now she was gone. I nodded my head.

He stood next to me, neither of us felt like saying anything. Finally I got to my feet and carefully folded the letter into my pocket.

'Are you ready to go back?'

I couldn't answer as the tears welled up again. I just shook my head.

'Would you prefer to be on your own tonight?'

Again I could only nod my head under the moon. He took a long deep lungful of air through his nostril and let it out slowly.

'Ann's private room will be cleaned out in the morning, there's a bed in there. I want you to be ready for the morning roll call at eight o'clock. Tomorrow morning, and everything returns to normal. This was Ann's wish, and I shall ensure it's carried out. The door to her balcony is unlocked and the duty officer has been told to stay away and not to mention it.'

Then he turned and walked back across the fields, disappearing in the darkness. Who knows what time it was when I finally dried my face . . . I didn't.

But when I had taken a last look across that river and walked away, I never went back there till the morning of the day I was due to leave for Birmingham. On that day, after one last look at the river, I threw Ann's letter into the waters and watched it float away. I could never have brought myself to destroy the letter and I couldn't have taken it with me for someone else to read.

Sedbury Park had taught me an awful lot. It had tried and tested me to the limits, and if I'm honest with myself, it helped to make me what I am now.

It made me tough, both physically and mentally. It taught me to cry when the walls of hell were pressing down on me. It taught me what love was, and what it was to belong, brief and painful though it was.

It taught me the backbreaking art of forestry, it taught me to build walls inside myself and outside for others. It taught me to span electricity cables and it taught me to span that chasm between myself and the rest of the world. It had even put me onto day work at the Chepstow end of the River Severn ferry that went across the river to Bristol. Here I learnt to make fast the incoming ferries before I could make fast my own life. It taught me the meaning of working with others behind you, but it never taught me how to be one of the boys. I have been, I am, and I suppose I always will be a loner of sorts. Until one day that special person comes along, and then the pain will begin again, and again I will lose them because they are in a hurry to get somewhere . . . I've already been.

The Governor was handing over my papers when I came in.

'Ahh, Dawson. Are you ready to leave?'

'Yes, Sir.'

'Good! This is Mr Newman and he's come down from Birmingham to take you to Coleshill school.'

For a moment I did't know what to do when the man held out his hand to me. I looked at it twice before reluctantly shaking hands with him. This was something new to me because the only hands which had ever been extended in my direction, were usually rolled up in the shape of a fist.

It was like shaking hands with a chunk of wood, that was how hard his hands were. If a nation is judged by the quality of it's Ambassador, then I was on my way to one hell of a tough establishment.

The man was devoid of any fat, his features honed down to the bone. He was wide and bone hard. And unknown to me at that time, he had been a Regimental Sergeant Major in the Royal Marine Commandos and was to become my guiding spirit until the day I also attained my Green Beret.

He lifted the already thick file from the desk, the file which represented my life whilst I walked the body out behind him. I stood for a moment under the high porch and looked across to the pilings of the new Severn Bridge. The sun was shining off the huge steel and concrete structures whilst the river of silver water flowed around them.

I looked around at the immense gardens surrounding the house, and remembered the long hours I'd spent wandering around them. The times I'd climbed in through the window of the fruit shed to steal apples. The long hours I'd spent in the school on my own with just one warden to watch over me during the Christmas holidays.

I thought about the triumph of collecting the elusive tin of Bill Eenys cigarette ends, and trading it. And I thought about Ann . . . dear Ann. I wondered where she was now. Yes, strangely enough I had liked this place, tough though it was. I still had the feeling it had been some kind of home for me.

Coleshall Approved School, after the sunny Bristol Channel, the clear sea air, the wide open spaces, the forests, and the ploughed fields; seemed the most depressing place on earth.

Built of red brick during the time of the Industrial Revolution, a purpose built detention centre, which looked more like a workhouse than even a prison. Dominating the three sided structure was a very large water tower, whose base also served as the main entrance. The interior of the building was made up of immense rooms with very high ceilings covering three floors. Whereas Sedbury Park still had the air and furnishings of a gentleman's house. Coleshall was a functional, no nonsense, barebones place of detention. One could imagine the homeless and out of work tramping the long corridors to and from their back breaking work for the rich owners. It was that kind of place.

As I followed Len Newman through the buildings towards the Governor's office, I could feel the hostile eyes of the inmates following me. And immediately I recognised a different kind of hostility. This was a hostility which was bred from the fear of outsiders, the fear that somehow you had changed into something ... different ... and you dared anyone to see it. You didn't want intruders. This was a closed society.

The Governor's office was a spacious woodpanelled affair split into two by a wood and glass screen. In the first half was the secretary's office which was manned by a red haired, tough, old lady. When Mr Newman asked to see the Governor, she rose from her seat and looked at me with the same hostility as that of the inmates.

'Is this the new arrival from Chepstow?'

She couldn't have shown more distain if she'd been eyeing a prospective clothes purchase.

'Hummm.'

She knocked on the glass door as a matter of courtesy and then marched in without waiting for an answer. It was obvious who thought they ran this place. She returned a few minutes later and held the door open for us.

'The Governor will see you now.'

He was a tall, dapper man dressed in the latest tight trousered fashion, his ginger hair close cropped to the head.

'Ahh, Mr Newman. You're back with the latest admission.'

He took the proffered file and sat down to study it, offering neither of us a seat. His study took him more than twenty minutes, at the end of which he dropped the file on the desk as if it was something unpleasant to touch.

'So, Dawson. Your reputation has preceeded you. You're already something of a celebrity. Two of your previous colleagues are here and have waxed lyrical about your toughness.'

Suddenly his hand slammed down on the desk, and the smile disappeared from his freckled face.

'Let me make a few things clear to you, Dawson. This is a much tougher place than the one you've been used to. The inmates here don't take too kindly to anyone who's already announced his arrival. Get into trouble here, there's no one to pull your chestnuts out of the fire. Get into a fight, and you're liable to get badly hurt. Cause any fights or disturbances, and I'm liable to come down on you like a ton of bricks. I run this place, not you and certainly not anyone else. Step out of line once, and you'll wish you'd never been born. You are here for one purpose only, that is to serve out the sentence that has been handed down to you. And then to go back out into the world and be a decent citizen. Do I make myself absolutely clear?'

The sweat beaded my forehead. This man made no bones about my position and that of the 'school'.

'Yes, sir.'

'Good. Then let's go through the rules. There's no smoking allowed except at the individual masters' discretion. Official smoking times are after lunch, and after the evening meal at six until bed time at nine o'clock. You're allowed two cigarettes a day and up to fourteen a week. Cigarettes and matches are handed out twice a day by the duty officer. The holding of any other stocks of tobacco is forbidden, and the trading of such, illegal.

'Your file says you have a bank account of nearly ten pounds. You're allowed to draw up to ten shillings a week of that money when you've earned the privilege of being allowed to go into the city. That privilege has to be earned, and is given when we're sure you have no desires to escape.

'You'll be given two shillings a week in pocket money, which you can use to buy sweets on a Friday night, or to buy tobacco. Any money which isn't spent has to be returned to your account of which you can keep a running total. The holding of money is illegal, as is using it to bribe or purchase favours.

'You are permitted visitors only after you've earned the privilege, and that usually takes about three months. In your case, I see it doesn't matter too much to you ... there's no one to visit you.

'You're allowed to receive as much mail as anyone wishes to send you, but it will be read first and if thought necessary ... censored ... with a pair of scissors. Should we not like the contents of any mail you receive, we hold the right to inform the sender that they are no longer allowed to write to you.

'You're allowed to receive food parcels from home and keep them in your private locker. The parcels will be opened first to ensure there's no files or escape equipment in them. Anyone sending food parcels should be advised not to put anything perishable in them.

Whilst you're here, you'll at all times wear the school uniform of khaki shorts and shirt in the summer, and long corduroy trousers and jacket in the winter. When you've earned the privilege to wear civilian clothes at the weekend you'll wear only those clothes issued to you by the school. Newspapers are allowed, only after they've been censored. There is a television here which you're allowed to watch for two hours a night. Radios are allowed during the free time as long as they are not a nuisance, but they are a privilige which has to be earned.

'We keep a system of marks here, and each week you're alloted seven marks, one for each day of the week. If you break any of the rules the marks will be deducted according to the severity of the offence. If by the end of three months you've sufficient marks, then the first of your privileges will be awarded. The rest to follow every seven days that you maintain your marks.

'The marks will be deducted for the following offences: fighting, trading, bribery, theft of school property, stealing an inmates property ... if he hasn't already broken your neck, being late, untidiness, being dirty when not necessary, untidy beds, holding of illegal stores and using them for illegal purposes, insubordination to an officer, failing to carry out an order and sloppy house work.

'Escaping, as in any of Her Majesty's detention establishments, is forbidden and dealt with severely. The punishment is twelve strokes of the cane, from three to seven days of solitary confinement with a diet of bread and water, a loss of all privileges for a month and no visits for three months. Plus ...

one to three months added onto your time.'

He studied my file again and then closed it.

'Your file says you've done forestry ... building ... electrical and general maintenance work. You also have some skills at operating a boiler system.'

'Yes, sir.'

'Good. We need people with experience.'

He looked to Mr Newman.

'His file says he has a desire to join the Royal Marines. I believe that's your field. Are you prepared to take him under your wing?'

Newman looked at me for a moment, calculating and assessing, I held my breath because he could make or break me.

'Yes, sir.'

The freckled face turned back to me.

'Good. I understand that the Royal Marines is a military service of extremely high standards, and one of the toughest. If you make it, then you'll have justified all the expectations we could have of you.

Mr Newman's department is gardening. You'll work under his guidance and learn all there is the know about it. Before you have left this place, you'll have gained a pracitcal and written UEI degree in horticultural botany, soils and manures ... any questions?'

One never asked the Governor questions, especially at the first interview. That was inviting trouble of the worst kind.

'No, sir.'

He smiled and jumped up. He was glad to see I'd learnt the rules of the game.

'Good. Then we understand each other. I hope there will be not further necessity to meet in this office again. Take him away, Mr Newman.'

As we walked along through the different departments to register, he told me the rest of the rules.

'The school is divided into three houses: White, Blue, and Red. You'll go into White House. That's my house. Dormitory on the top floor. Once a week there is a boot and shoe inspection on the parade ground, plus a wandering inspection every day. For the first three months you'll do house work like the rest here, then when you get your priviliges we'll see what other work is available. Rise at six, wash inspection every morning after the house work is done, breakfast at seven, normal days work starts at eight. Lunch at 12.30 to 13.00, smoking time to 13.30. Back to work, finish at 16.30, tea and then supper at 20.00. Bed at 21.00. Understood?'

There were more rules and regulations here than could be absorbed in one go.

'I think so.'

He suddenly turned round and called a short stocky boy who was walking along the corridor.

'Alberici. come here.'

Yes,sir.'

'His name's Dawson. Transfer from Chepstow. He's on your table. Show him the ropes, and if he makes a mistake I'm going to have your guts for garters. clear?'

'Yes, sir.'

Newman was gone before I could turn round.

'So, you're Dawson!'

He looked me up and down as if he was measuring to see whether I lived up to my apparent reputation.

'Heard you're a mean fighter.'

'Sorry. I can't help what other people say.'

'You'll have to watch yourself for a while. Anyone who's got a few nuts loose is going to call you out for a fight. And there's quite a few of them here . . . they think they're the local John Waynes.'

He wasn't being nasty or anything. He was just stating a fact. The moment a newcomer came into the place, someone would pick a fight with him, usually at the insistence of one of the senior boys. The dirtiest and the meanest fighters would be chosen for the task, just to test the metal of the newcomer, and to establish his position in the school hierarchy. Anyone who refused to fight, would be branded a coward and sent into internal exile and the ridicule of the whole place. A good fight and you were respected. If you won the fight, then the next challenger would come after you until you had worked your way up to the top of the ladder. It was very bad policy to win the first fight unless you were seriously provoked, and very bad policy to lose it.

Alberici turned out to be a respectable chap. He neither bullied nor harrassed anyone. There was no fighting over the food on the table, everyone getting his fair share of what was available. And when something needed explaining, he explained it.

My first job the following morning turned out to be the dirtiest job in the school. Cleaning out the school toilets. There were three of us on the job, and the senior of the boys was glad to move up to another job. Before we had even got started, there was a commotion and a sharp order to "Keep Watch". A struggling and screaming figure was dragged into one of the urinals and beaten to the sound of curses, punches and kicks. Whilst two of them held him down, his head in a bowl of pee, the other one peed over his face. Another final beating and he was left on the floor.

'Anyone see anything?'

It was an aggressive challenge. We went back to our mopping out as if nothing had happened. The others quickly left and the one on the floor crawled away. Justice was swift and hard in this place.

The challenge came three days later. For a while I'd noticed someone kept following me around at a distance. At the breakfast table that morning, I'd asked Alberici who it was. He looked carefully to the one indicated, and sighed.

'That's Chesterton. He's the school boxer. Boxes against lads from other approved schools. Gained a licence from the Amateur Boxing Association last year and is allowed to box in outside tournaments. Is he after you?'

'I think so. He keeps giving me the evil eye.'

'You'd better watch yourself with him. He's got a few nuts loose at the best of times. He's liable to catch you at the worst moment when you can't defend yourself.'

'Who's backing him?'

'The three most senior in the school. They're the oldest and have been here the longest.'

'But I'm no threat to them. They're five years older than me and twice my size.'

'Who're you kidding. You're growing by the day. Anyway ... that's not important. What is important is the following. Winter's coming.

'What? Winter? What the hell's that got to do with this?'

Alberici sighed as if he was talking to a backward pupil.

'Oh, boy. Have you got a lot to learn. Do you play table

tennis? Snooker? Billiards? Dominos? Read comics, play cards and sit on hot radiators? Watch television? Watch the film once a week during the winter?'

He looked at me, the penny still hadn't dropped.

'Four can play table tennis. Two, snooker and billiards. Any amount Dominos. There is only a limited amount of unread material in this place and twenty hot radiators in the day room to keep the place warm. And the front four rows of chairs are the only ones worth watching television from. You'll only get a place if the top echelon is doing something else.'

The penny had dropped. If I wanted a place in any of these things then I was going to have to fight for it. There was no way I was going to get out of it.

'How do I take him?'

'Watch your back, and go in hard and fast the moment he gets near you. Keep well clear of his head, he likes to butt with it. Whatever you do, don't injure him or else you've got more trouble.'

Everybody has to go to the toilet sometime, and that's where he caught me. With my trousers down. The door came flying open and he stormed in.

'You've been telling everyone your a hard nut. I say you're a liar.'

It's damned difficult to fight with your trousers down and I had to use my foot to fend him off until I could get prepared. My hands were just free when he came at me, fists up and lips drawn back over the gap where the three front teeth were missing. It was plain to see he was a boxer. Three fast blows caught me on the side of the head before I could do anything, I was seeing stars. He closed in and I saw his head go back for the head butt. Forestry work is a bone hard job, and after a while it begins to tell on your physique. I had finished felling and trimming twenty trees only a week before . . . with a five pound axe.

I ducked inside his guard and caught his belt and shoulder and heaved him from the ground, dropped him down onto my knee and heard the air scream out of his lungs. He was fit and was on his feet very fast. He closed again and this time I had to use my fists and my weight. He went backwards, and I had him against the door. Knee to the groin, two into the stomach. I fought out of fear that I might not be able to stop him, and he would get the better of me.

He was a hard fighter, that I must say. But somehow luck favoured me that day. He went down, and I kept going in.

In a fighting ring, and under rules, I could never have beaten him, but this was a different sort of fighting.

I stood back, chest heaving, sweat pouring our of me. I'd remembered Alberici words 'If you beat him and he's down, back off immediately. Don't add insult to injury, the people at the top will respect you for it more. And when you walk away don't run.'

I hadn't realised to now that we had an audience. There were more than twenty inmates crowded into the place, one or two older ones, and obviously runners for the senior boys. This was the moment when things could go wrong if anyone decided to avenge Chesterton. I headed towards Alberici at a steady pace, he was stood at the front and when I got close he stood back to let me through, the rest finally decided to follow suit.

Supper was a casual affair of hot cocoa, full of bromine, and a sandwich. This was the only meal we were not forced to eat. It was rarely turned down. Alberici came and stood next to me.

'Where did you learn to handle yourself like that?'

'Picked it up on the way.'

'You've been to a few hard schools.'

I nodded my head.

'Is that it now? Does it stop now?'

I really didn't want to fight. I was getting tired of it.

'Unless Chesterton decides to take it personally, then I think you've got your place on the radiators.'

His voice dropped and he lifted the mug to his lips to hide what he was saying.

'He's behind you. Watch yourself. I can't see his intentions.'

I swung around to face him, the bruise under his eye was quite livid. I could still feel where his blows had landed on me. The room went quiet, they were waiting. I transferred my cocoa to my left hand, slowly, so as not to give the wrong impression, then stuck out my hand to him. He was reluctant, the light of hatred in his eyes. Someone standing behind nudged him in the back and slowly he took my hand. The tension subsided, his respect was saved. As Alberici had said

'You don't kick a dog when he's down.'

After that, I found it a lot easier to settle into the routine and structure of the place.

5

The first three months passed relatively quietly as autumn turned to winter, and everything began to become covered in what seemed more like permafrost. One degree below freezing, trying to scrub flagsone corridors and verandas on one's hands and knees with buckets of cold water soon began to take toll amongst the inmates. Very often we would have to attend the daily surgery with a variety of complaints ranging from swollen knees from kneeling on the frozen ground, to chapped and cracked hands from squeezing water from near frozen floor cloths. The regimen was hard, very hard. There was no let up regardless of whether it rained, hailed, or the sun shone.

We'd stand, every morning, half naked in the freezing driving snow or rain, waiting for the inspection line to decrease in size and bring us a little nearer to the warm wash room and the inspecting officer: whose tempers we'd learnt to guage according to the state of the moon and time of day.

I had finally learnt all the menial cleaning jobs in the school, and on the final day of my three month probation period was grandly informed by Len Newman that I was to take command of the gardening department's boiler system.

This was a job of some considerable responsibility, as, during the winter the department was responsible for supplying the school with a certain amount of fresh vegetables which were grown in the warmed greenhouses. It meant getting up fifteen minutes earlier than the rest of the school, and then shovelling half a ton of coke into the boiler house to keep the boiler going for the rest of the day. It also meant working up to eight-thirty at night to keep a steady fire going so that the warm water system didn't begin to cool off.

Whether I was given this job because of Len Newman's choice, or because I was the only one available for it, I shall never know. What I do know, is that the young man who was doing the job at the moment was about to leave the school in two weeks and I was supposed to learn the job.

Surprisingly, even this job was not immune from acts of sabotage. Acts usually carried out by someone who was aggrieved by something you said, did, a glance, or even jealousy, because they hadn't got the job they thought they were entitled to.

Such was the case now. Someone, within the school, was very upset that I'd been given the boiler job. Almost before my predecessor had been gone from the school twenty-four hours, trouble began. It was my job to maintain a steady temperature from the coke fired boilers raking out old ashes, building the fire slowly, feeding it and then keeping it going for the next four months . . . without it once going out.

We had more than 4,000 quadratmetres of heated greenhouses, all functioning and fed by a system of valves and wheel gates which I had to open and close manually with boring regularity.

I had been solely in command of these boilers for exactly twenty-four hours, when Len Newman stood at the foot of my bed, breathing fire.

'Dawson. The bloody boilers are out. Stone cold.'

I was coming out of the bed like greased lightning, grabbing my clothes and dragging them on.

'But, sir. When I left the boilers last night, they were banked up and burning well.'

His head was barely a metre away as he breathed down my neck.

'Oh, yes. They were burning so well, they burnt themselves out before midnight. You can only be grateful it wasn't so cold last night. How many times were you told to close the ventilators on the boilers before closing down for the night?'

I stopped for a minute. The ventilators? But they were closed. I had made sure they were closed . . . or had I?

'You get yourself down there, Dawson. Or else you'll be in trouble.'

Len Newman was a man with chiselled features, and penetrating eyes. And when he got angry . . . you weren't left with any doubt as to his anger ... I was dragging on my clothes and running out of the dormitory.

There was no way I would get any breakfast this morning, because the boilers would take at least an hour to fire up and then at least another hour of careful attention before they would produce any real heat.

As I ran down the path towards the gardening department, my mind was in turmoil as I tried to analyse every move which had been made when I'd shut down for the night. For the life of me I couldn't possibly come up with an answer. I kept on thinking about what I'd been taught, and wondered if perhaps my predecessor had been playing tricks on me.

I ran down the steps into the boiler house, and could feel the cool air. Normally this place was warm, and in spite of its permanent coating of coke dust, a rather cosy place ... when it was cleaned ... and warm. I looked down at the ventilators which were used to draw air over the fire and make it burn faster ... they were open!

I quickly checked the main return valves and found one of them was closed. It meant that the water would not have been able to circulate in the huge pipes and so would have overheated the greenhouses, and with falling temperatures the temperature differences would be quite considerable. How could I have made such a mistake?

I set to cleaning out the old ashes, pulling them on to the floor at my feet and then trampling over them, because there was no way I could take time to clear them away, it was too important that the inside of the boiler didn't get too cold.

I quickly closed the in and out wheel gates to trap the water in the boiler so it would warm faster, and then set about relighting the fire. There was no wood. Now, I was sure I'd cut an emergency stock of wood for just such and event ... but had I? I had to go into the tool shed to find some wooden cases which I could use as firewood.

The fire crackled and glowed, lifted and died, to rise from the ashes and began to burn with a certain amount of determination.

I watched the water temperature gauge slowly falling as I cursed the fire into action. But it took more than an hour for the huge twenty-four leaf boiler to begin to catch the falling water temperature and then lift it up to a more acceptable level, from which point I was able to slowly reopen the wheel valves.

I was wiping my hands on an old rag which hung from my overall pocket when I heard Len Newman's limping stride come down the steps. He quickly checked all the guages to see that the temperatures and pressures hadn't fallen too far.

'The next time you let that fire out, there'll be hell to pay. If you can't do the job, then say so. In the meantime, get yourself cleaned up and get some breakfast.'

He turned his back on me and stomped out of the boiler house. I was depressed because I'd let him down, and promised myself that this would the last time and that I'd be doubly careful in the future, until I'd reached the point where I could do the job in my sleep.

The next incident occured at the weekend, three days later, and this time it was Len Newman's second officer and fellow gardening colleague who pulled me from the bed.

Mr Wheeler was a very tall, well built man who'd spent a long time in the deserts of Africa during the Second World War. He was as gentle as a lamb, and had a temperement to go with it. But when he got upset, everyone kept a long way away from his spade like hands which could hit with force and speed. And this time there was the glint of anger in his eyes as he stood at the foot of my bed, the foot of the bed being suspended above the floor by about two feet. I was looking up hill at the tall well built man with the close cropped curly hair. Suddenly he let the bed fall to the wooden floor boards and I could feel my teeth rattle with the vibration.

'You'd better get down to those boilers before Mr Newman gets his hands on you. They're out, and the place is full of water. It was also cold enough last night for us to have lost one complete greenhouse full of vegetables.'

I could hardly find words to express my surprise, I had been so careful the night before. I couldn't waste time thinking about how it had happened, I could hear Len Newman's voice getting closer, and it wasn't something which I wished to confront right now. I thought I'd made it as I ran for the back stairs, and then suddenly I was brought to a skidding halt as the military voice of Len Newman cut across the entire length of the dormitory.

'Dawson! Stay right were you are. Where the hell do you

think you're slinking off to?'

I turned slowly to face him.

'Ummm . . . well . . .Mr Wheeler told me . . .'

'And what did he tell you. I hope he told you that your life is very short, and is about to end in the next few minutes.'

Len Newman's determined limp carried him across the dormitory in a very deliberate fashion. There was a look on his face which I wasn't too sure about.

'Dawson. You've got some explaining to do . . . but later. I want you down to the boiler house and I want the mess cleaned up. Fire up the system and top up the water level. You'll have to stay there and bleed the air out as the temperature rises . . . This time you'd better not make any more mistakes.'

When I reached the boiler house, my heart fell to the floor and slid under the boiler itself. There was at least two feet of water around the boiler, which had effectively put out the fire. I slumped down on the steps and looked at the dust laden oily black water. It was not possible that I'd made another mistake, I had been extra careful since the last incident. I could remember well that before closing the system down for the previous night I had carefully checked the ventilators, the setting of the valves and wheel gates, the temperature settings and the amount of coke that was on the fire. I'd even shovelled the half ton of coke that was required for the following morning into the boiler house so that it would be dry and warm, making for easier combustion.

Suddenly I looked to the far wall and saw that the previous night's efforts were submerged under the black water. There wasn't even dry coke to start the next fire.

As I sat looking dejectedly at the mess, an idea began to grow in my head which I didn't like the sound of. I didn't want to allow the idea room in my head, but I couldn't get rid of it. I stood up and walked down into the cold water, without the benefit of even a pair of wellingtons which would have filled with water and made movement very difficult. I groped around in the water looking for the main outlet valve which was situated at the foot of the heating unit. When my fingers touched it, I felt a little scared to test my theory, because I knew that if I was right, then things would never be the same again.

I took a deep breath and bent down a little further until my hand grabbed the full width of the wheel, I was wet up to the waist, my clothes acting like a sponge . . . but it didn't matter. I twisted the wheel right and felt it give . . . it was open . . . someone had deliberately opened it . . . it had been sabotaged.

The realisation of the situation made me feel sick in the stomach, but it also made me resolute. Someone hated me . . . but who? . . . and more importantly . . . why?

I didn't have time to think about reasons, I had go get the mess cleaned up. I went down onto my hands and knees and literally groped my way across the boiler house floor until I could find the grating which covered the drain.

As I had begun to suspect, it had been stopped up with earth and old rags.

I pulled blindly at the stuff, throwing each item across the room onto the concrete steps, I only hoped that Len Newman would believe me. But why should he? He was no different to the other jailers. They only believed what they saw, their imagination ending the moment they opened the first door in the morning. But I wanted him to believe . . . I needed him to believe . . . because I trusted him!

The water rushed down into the drainage system leaving a dirty black smudge over everything it had touched, including myself. Just then the room was darkened as two figures descended the concrete steps. Slowly I stood up and faced the two stern faced men who ran the gardening department.

'Well, Dawson. You'd better have some good answers for this.'

Len Newman passed his hand around the boiler house.

'I gave you this chance because Ann Summers wrote to me personally, she begged me to give you a chance. Ever since you've had the job we've had nothing but trouble . . . my personal opinion . . . is that you've got a grudge against us . . . for some reason or other you don't like us. And you think that if you make trouble, then perhaps we'll notice you or you'll get sent to some other place. I'm here to tell you Dawson, that you're here to stay. And if you think you're going to get into the Royal Marines then you can think again.'

The two big men stepped down from the steps, slowly advancing on me. Panic rose in my throat as I watched them come. I was desperately looking for answers . . . I knew there would be a beating coming . . . a private beating . . . out of eye and hearing.

'Errr . . . I . . . I . . . found the outlet valve . . . open. I mean . . . it was open . . . simply open. The water came from there.'

Len Newman stood in front of me, his eyes were steady.

'What time did you come down here during the night?' I gave a nervous laugh . . . his question and ideas were so . . . plausible. I wondered whether he would be trying to make me believe them.

'I. . . I didn't come down here. The . . . err . . . the dormitories are always locked at night.'

'What time did you stoke the boilers for the last time?'

'Err . . . I think . . . about 20.15. Then I went back and had supper . . . and bed.'

The two men looked hard at me. I stumbled on . . . I wanted Len Newman to believe me. Suddenly it was important to me.

'Those rags there, and the soil . . . they were stuffed into the drain stopping the water from running away . . . the valve was opened, deliberately, so that the water ran out of the pipes and built up until it doused the fire.'

The two men stood looking at the mess, the rags and the earth which now lay in a heap near the now clear drain. They looked down at their stained wellingtons and finally at me. I could see the doubt in their eyes . . . especially those of Len Newman. Finally he spoke.

'Get changed and have breakfast. Then clean up this mess with the fire hose, dry the boiler out with a fire and then get the thing functioning. I want the temperature back up to normal by 10 o'clock this morning . . .'

He turned to leave, and for a moment I took a deep breath.

'. . . I'll be appointing someone else to run the boilers. They'll be giving you a hand. I'll take care of their training myself. Tomorrow morning you can report to the duty officer who will appoint you a house cleaning job.'

The words drove the life out of my body. How could he . . . the person I so much trusted . . . refuse to believe me. How could he think that I'd sabotaged my own duties. A job which had so many privileges, a job that was so much sought after. I was dreaming . . . but of course . . . it was just a dream.

I pinched myself hard as I watched the two men disappear up the steep concrete steps. But they didn't vanish in a puff of smoke, only their footsteps lingered in the air.

I was mortified that Len Newman would think I'd deliberately sabotaged my own work. Someone, somewhere, had it in for me. Perhaps they didn't like me personally, or perhaps they had a grudge against the gardening department, or ... and a more likely reason ... they didn't like the fact that I'd got a favoured job after only three months of being in the place. As I changed out of my wet clothes and put on gardening overalls before walking back to the school, I thought about the privileges which my job had given me.

I was not required to attend the early morning wash inspections. And I was excused all house cleaning duties. Being on boiler duty, I could smoke when I wanted to without fear of being caught. I was excused attending meal times if the boilers needed attention, and I could, if necessary, be late to bed. Enviable priviliges in a restricted society. Who was after them? Someone who felt that the job should have gone to them.

But there was no way I would ever find out who was responsible. In such a closed society as that which I was living in, nobody ever passed on rumours about their colleagues, and if they did and were found out ... the price was very high.

Instead, I could only watch my back and the next morning I started the potato detail. Again, it was a job with privileges, but, this time it was a job nobody wanted ... but nobody.

The job required me to peel and prepare approximately fifty kilos of potatoes each morning ... with the aid of a peeling machine ... and then present them to the chef for approval. He was a small man, with a big man trying to squeeze it's way out of him. He had a foul temper and used it to sarcastic excellence on the unfortunate who was given the potato cleaning detail.

Christmas was arriving on an express train, and the inmates were getting excited. Applications were being submitted to the Govenor every single day as letters were received from parents and relatives saying they would accept responsibility for their kin during the holiday if the Governor would release him.

Confidential Government reports would be consulted to see whether the guarantors were considered unworthy for such a task. And then . . . two weeks before the holidays were due to start, a list would be pinned to the noticeboard. The list was of all those who had been granted a parole for the Christmas period.

As can be imagined, 120 caged animals watched the board each day waiting for the crucial list, circling each other as they moved into position to be able to see the list of names first. When it arrived, there was fighting, tears, and shocked silence from those whose name wasn't on it. Then masses of letters would be dashed off asking for the families to apply for parole permission.

Each day the list would be added to and as each name appeared there would be jubilation and untold amounts of bragging as to what the named persons would be doing when they got home.

I found myself studying the list with a hammering heart and falling hopes, until one day I found out that at Christmas there would be only one inmate enjoying Christmas behind the locked doors of Coleshill School . . . and that was me.

Excitement became rife as the day for departure approached. It was a tangible thing which couldn't be ignored as old emnities and all bartering debts were forgotten. Nobody, but nobody, would take even the slightest element of risk with their parole. Everybody walked carefully around their friends and enemies alike, refusing to be drawn into anything that would risk the parole.

Even the wardens would turn a blind eye to the rare infringements of the establishment rules. They too wanted to enjoy Christmas with their families rather than having to stand duty time.

There was no other time in my life which hurt so much as Christmas . . . this one especially. Even inmates whom I'd had little or no contact with, would espress their sympathy with me. And one boy with whom I'd made good friends said he would ask his parents if they would take me for Christmas. I had refused his offer with the excuse that it would never be allowed. Because I couldn't tell him I was too scared to approach the Governor knowing the shattering blow of a possible refusal would be more than I could bear. And there was something deeper, I was scared to open the door to the outside world in case the outside world slammed the door on me because I was too . . . alien.

Three days before Christmas, and on the day of departure, the excitement in the place was almost unbearable. I could feel myself choking on it, I fought for breath, and found myself sitting in the darkest holes of the building unable to face what was going on around me. The loneliness tore at every fibre of my body, as it drove me into the depths of hell. Never before in my short life had I felt so unwanted . . . and not belonging.

Every time one of the inmates saw me, there would be an embarrassed moment of silence and they would ask if they could bring something back for me. I would silently shake my head and fight like hell to hold back the tears. Even the offer of friendship and help had to be rejected, the hope that went with it was more than could be tolerated.

The first of the parents and relatives arrived at nine o'clock that morning. Hopes and fears soared amongst the inmates as they watched with expectations the approaching cars.

I was appointed to direct the parents to the dining room where they had to sign a book accepting the responsibility for their charges. It was the most brutal of tortures as I watched the vehicles arrive, the adults trooping into the dining room and then departing happily with their charges. By eleven o'clock most of the inmates had gone, and those who were left waiting, sat with shattered nerves as the clock ticked by.

At twelve-thirty I closed the main door on the last of the adults and walked with the heaviest heart back into the silent building. I could still hear the voices of the inmates lingering in the air, the laughter, the curses, the incessant hope and dejection. Wherever I walked in the massive building it followed me, mocking, hurting, tearing at me. A door, a sound, an empty room, a familiar face no longer there.

I found myself standing in the huge wash room, a place which until now, had always been the focal point of the place. It was silent . . . cold . . . and deserted. Sounds and voices bounced off the tiled walls, faces were reflected in the mirrors, silent taps gurgled with water and I stood totally alone.

I wished that all the forces of hell would destroy me and knew I would enjoy the painful moments before oblivion . . .

but at least it would be over.

It was the old white haired warden who found me some time later sitting on the cold concrete floor, tears spent, body drained. He was without a family and had been appointed to look after me for the next two weeks. He demanded nothing of me, and equally gave nothing. Sometimes he cooked a meal, and sometimes I did. Then he would sit in front of the television, leaving me to wander the vast complex alone.

On Christmas Day I had to run to the deepest bowels of the building to get away from the sound of Christmas carols being sung on the television which was never switched off. Each cord which was sung, built pictures of happy families in my mind. And each chord which was sung hammered down the nails of loneliness and rejection into my body. Long hours were spent wandering in the bitter cold, going nowhere, each nook and cranny bringing back painful memories of better days . . . I would have willingly and happily given up life . . . had I known how to.

6

They trickled back slowly. The first arrivals were at the main door by nine o'clock on the Saturday morning. They came in sheepishly, strangely. They smelt and moved with the contamination of the outside world. Unsure of themselves, trying to hide their unease with unnecessary bravado. The shaded looks at their families as they tried to hide their embarrassment. Mothers, fathers, sisters, brothers, aunts, uncles . . . grandparents. They all came, some even came with the family pets. And they all stood around, uttering soothing words to each other, but each one clearly uncomfortable in this strange atmosphere.

The duty officers met each arrival and relieved the charges of all money and cigarettes before they were allowed back into the establishment. Food parcels were searched to see that there was no contraband, and then allowed to be packed away in the personal lockers in the day room.

The goodbyes were both short and long, some genuine and some forced. Tears flowed as girlfriends played their parts, and mothers fretted over their respective sons. And all the time, I wished they hadn't come back. I liked the memories better than I liked the fact, the silence of the place had become a better friend to me than all those who were returning.

But as the day wore on, a certain excitement began to invade the place. There was a very strict government rule that said, anyone who failed to return by six o'clock in the evening, would be considered an escapee. The names and numbers were being ticked off as the clock ticked by, and bets were already being laid as to who would fail to return. But as the clock struck six, the last name was crossed off and the doors were closed again to the outside world. Supper was served, but very few took the meal.

The inmates were subdued, but loud in bragging about their exploits, the girls they'd been in bed with, and the crimes they'd committed whilst outside. The truth of the matter being that few had stepped outside the parole rules, their parents satisfying their every need.

It took more than a week of bullying and cajoling by the wardens to get the school back into it's settled ways. There were fights a-plenty as the order of hierarchy had to be re-established, it had changed, and I found myself placed quite highly in it ... and yet, I was placed outside it ... I now occupied a very special place in the school. Something had happened during the Christmas period which took me some time to understand ... I had grown up, very painfully, beyond my years, and the world looked a lot different. Inmates who had shunned me before, were deferential to me. Those who hadn't even noticed that I existed, suddenly saw me. I'd spent two weeks of my life in conditions of solitary confinement, and survived it. No mercy had been shown to me, and no mercy was expected. In such a society, it was something which deserved, and got, much respect.

I was never again called upon to defend my position in the school, but all those around me rose and fell according to their abilities to survive. I had earned a place within the society that I lived, but within the world at large, I was an even bigger nothing. What could I tell the world about myself? A world that measured everything by its pedigree ... Nothing!

I was now fourteen years of age and knew less about where I came from than a five-year-old child. And it was troubling me to the point where I was choking on it. I wanted so much to belong somewhere, to someone. To someone whom I could look up to and measure my progress in life. There was no one, and it was eating away inside of me. Then one day I took the courage in my hands and faced Len Newman.

'Sir. I want to know where I come from.'

We stood in the middle of a frozen, snow covered track, me with my feet planted wide, determined and reckless.

'Why is it so important to you?'

I was frightened. I was on a course for which there was no turning back, and I knew there would only be trouble at the end of it. Nobody could challenge the system and expect to come away from it unscathed. But what had I to lose? He was the only person I could talk to. I needed him to understand me . . . how I needed him to understand.

'Because I'm scared . . . I'm scared of the secrets . . . of the uncertainty. I need to know from where I come.'

'You've already tried. And it brought you only trouble. Why can't you leave it? You're on a collision course with the Governor . . . and only you will be the loser.'

'Sir . . .'

My head was filled with masses of words, filling it until I was confused, not knowing the right way to go. But I was committed . . . was it so wrong to want to know who you were?

'I can't take it anymore . . . the uncertainty . . . the feeling of helplessness . . . the hopelessness. I have this feeling of being . . . adrift. I need to know where I come from. I need to know who my parents are. Where they come from. I need to gain . . . I need an identity . . . I want something to hold on to. I want someone out there to say he's mine . . . I claim him . . . he's my flesh and blood. I must come from somewhere.'

'But you are yourself. What does it matter where you come from. What matters is where you're going. You have the possibility of a unique future ahead of you. Why mess it up with things which can't help you?'

And suddenly the world became very clear to me. He knew. He knew, or at least he'd tried to find out.

'Who am I?'

He lit a cigarette and took his time to fill his lungs. Indecision was clearly written on his face.

'I suggest you drop this matter . . . in fact, I'm telling you to drop it.'

'I can't. I walk through this place as if I'm in a dream. I listen to the mail calls, my head screaming out for recognition . . . a letter . . . a card . . . something. I watch the arrival of the parents on visiting day and feel like I'm no part of this world. Two years and never once a letter or a visitor . . . nothing . . . nothing . . . nothing . . .'

I was committed, I needed him to understand . . . I wanted him to understand.

'. . . I can't sleep at night anymore. There are many nights when I lie awake and stare at the ceiling . . . unable to close my eyes, because I fear that when I wake up, the little I have now . . . will be gone. The only memories I have are of the constant beatings and brutality . . . I always seem to create anger in every adult I meet . . . I never ever seem to do the right thing. When I do sleep, I have nightmares of drifting on an open sea . . . of falling . . . forever falling down a long unending tunnel . . . I'm frightened . . . I'm frightened because I know I'm losing control . . . I'm helpless . . . desperately.'

'You were told in Chepstow that your parents are dead.'

How could I explain to him that burning feeling inside of me . . . that feeling which said it was all lies . . . the feeling which told me that somewhere out there was my mother and father.

'They're not. I know it deep inside of myself that they're not.'

'You're on dangerous ground, Dawson. We're not in the habit of lying. You've been told what has been considered good for you.'

'Do you believe it, sir?'

It took him a few minutes to answer. I could see his mind was in turmoil.

'Is this an official request?'

His tone of voice had changed, he was no longer a friend. He was a man carrying out his job. He was a warden dealing with a difficult prisoner. I was risking everything, but the loyalty to someone out there, was inside of me.

'Yes, sir.'

'Be at the Governor's office in one hour. This will go down on your record . . . I warn you it will not help you.'

Then he was gone, and I could feel the weight of the world pressing down on me. I had lost a friend, of that I was sure.

I stood in the hall outside the Governor's office, trying not to notice the sidelong glances from the inmates as they passed by. Waiting outside the Governor's office at this time of day was bad news. I was so frightened I could feel my heart beat choking me . . . the Governor was a man who dealt harshly with anyone who refused to accept an official ruling.

The door opened and the school secretary beckoned me in, another bad sign. I followed her into the carpeted office and stood before the Governor's desk. There was a set routine when facing the Governor and I had difficulty in getting the words out, the hostility in the air was a tangible thing.

'Dawson ... err ... No. 73 ... white house. On the gardening detail.'

It was forbidden to look directly at the Governor, I could only look at a space above his head. The man's silence was unnerving me. Even though Len Newman was standing next to the Governor, I couldn't see him, such was the awe-inspiring power of the Governor.

'Dawson. When you were in Chepstow, you went for a psychiatric test. Do you know what the result of that test was?'

'I ... I ... no, sir.'

I could hear the ruffling of papers, and then one was chosen from the thick file on the desk. He read from it.

'It is the considered opinion that the patient has a persecuted complex. He assumes that his superiors are deliberately lying to him, and he refuses to accept the authority of those whose job it is to watch over him. The patient has delusions of grandeur which are incompatible with his background. It is the considered opinion of the examining panel, that this patient is mentally disturbed and at some time in the future will have to be subjected to treatment in a psychiatric unit ...

'Mr Newman has taken great pains to explain everything to me what you said. What do you have to say?'

There are no words to describe the shattering, crushing blow which the Governor had dealt me. I felt myself, my confidence, my whole being slowly crumbling around me. Tears coursed down my cheeks and I was helpless to stop them. I struggled to get the words out.

'I have ... I have nothing ... to say sir.'

I could hardly bear the silence ... he could shout and scream ... but I needed to get out of the office. I needed to be somewhere else ... I had to live with the verdict which had been passed on me ... no ... I was crazy.

'What right do you think you have, to question the painstaking official investigation that was carried out to discover your background! It was done to settle the question of your background once and for all! ... and here you are again ... stirring up trouble, and refusing to believe anything which

is told you by those in a position to know better than you.
Your parents are dead! Do you understnd me, Dawson? Dead!
You were taken into custody when there was no one else to
look after you. You were born a Bastard . . . to unmarried
parents . . . neither of whom are living now. That is the result
of the official investigation . . . and you seem hell-bent on
refusing to believe it . . . And another thing. What right do
you think you have asking one of my officers to pass a personal
judgement on an official report?'

Len Newman, the man whom I'd trusted had dealt me a
devastating blow. The man whom I had felt I could trust . . .
had destroyed me. I couldn't get any words out of my throat
. . . I was totally unable to answer.

A fist hammered down on the desk.

'I want an answer, Dawson!'

I was choking on my own sobs, the destruction within me
becoming total. Whatever happened I had to try and maintain
some dignity . . . I couldn't break down . . . not here . . . not
in front of Len Newman. Surely they could understand that?

'I will take your silence as insolence, and a challenge to the
authority of this office . . .'

He looked up at me, waiting for an answer, but my throat
refused to work. I was in complete shock.

The file was slammed to.

'Three days solitary confinement and one month on your
sentence. Take him away, Mr Newman. Sentence to start
immediately, a diet of stale bread and water.'

I could have been walking to my own death at the gallows
for all I knew. Each step I took as I was forced to walk ahead
of Len Newman seemed like a step towards a private hell. By
the time I reached the first floor and the solitary confinement
cells, the matron was standing there waiting. She gave me a
cursory examination and pronounced me fit to serve my
sentence . . . and then the door was closed on me.

I cannot, and will not, attempt to explain what the solitary
confinement cell meant to me this time. I only know that I
suffered and experienced the absolute depths of despondency
and crushing psychological pain interspersed with periods of
mental oblivion. No crime ever committed can justify the
inhuman treatment of being shut in a cell which deprives a
human being of all sight and sound of his existence. No crime

ever committed can equal the dehumanizing crushing oblivion which the solitary confinement cell represents. And it's use is a sign of the inhuman inflexiblity of those who are the first to call themselves civilised people. If I knew that one day I would have to face the inside of such a cell again, then I would prefer the dignity of death, than the sound of that door being locked behind me.

There were no smiles from the inmates when I was discharged from the solitary confinement. Instead, there were covert looks and a deliberate effort to avoid contact with me. They were frightened, frightened of me. They were frightened that if they were seen to favour me with their company, then one warder or the other would descend upon them, and they too would be serving time in solitary confinement. They feared contamination from someone who'd been singled out for persecution, and I couldn't blame them. Each one had a family, or friends waiting for them in the outside world, and extra time was like a death sentence. The solitary confinement cell meant a loss of privileges, a loss of contact with the outside world, a total cut off of all food parcels, mail, visits, cigarettes, pocket money and all work privileges ... it was a death sentence for an inmate.

This state of affairs was never again to change for me and things were never allowed to return to their former status. I was not rejected by the inmates, but they weren't prepared to accept the risk of association. I was left to my own devices, and as I again adjusted to my new situation, the inmates breathed a sigh of relief and settled down to their separate lives.

That is, until one day when I was approached by two of the senior inmates during my daily job of peeling the quota of potatoes. They stood in the doorway of the old brick building that had one time served as a grain store, which even on the hottest day was cool and slightly damp.

I was dressed in a rubber apron and wellingtons, and waded through the water which cascaded across the floor from the old peeling machine.

'We want you to join the escape committee?'

The tall, dark haired youth who was the senior of all inmates, seemed as though he was swallowing something a little distasteful.

'I think you're talking to the wrong person. My name's Dawson, I'm the one who always ends up in solitary confinement. You've even turned my stay here into a form of solitary confinement.'

The two of them looked at each other, then came inside the dark, damp, building. They obviously didn't want to be seen talking to me.

'That's why we think it would be a good idea for you to join the committee. The screws here won't be expecting you to be part of it.'

'I don't know anything about escaping. I've only done it once, and then I had to go to the police because my partner was injured. The sort of escaping you're talking about now, is not the kids stuff I was involved in. You're talking about the highly sophisticated, long distance run and then submergence in a large city ... I'm afraid I don't have any experience of that.'

There was a moment of silence, and I knew what was coming.

'But you've already won an award for field craft and manoeuvres with the cadets, and you are the unit's Sergeant, so, you're certainly not without experince.'

I turned back towards the machine, and opened it to let the potatoes fly out into the dustbin which was used to transport them to the school. Only experience had taught me exactly where to place the dustbin, so that every potato would land in the bin without me having to go through the laborious job of switching off the machine. What he had said was true.

Within three months of me being in the school, I'd been recruited into the Army Cadet unit that the school was quite well known for. It was part of a larger combined unit of cadets, which came under the watchful eye of the regular army and the Ministry of Defence.

The purpose of these units was to acquaint young impressionable kids with a sense of life in the British army. Because the army is a volunteer army, it has to rely heavily on goodwill, the sense of duty to the country and, most important of all, a surfeit of the rogue element within a poor society. I had fitted the requirements of this unit exceedingly well.

Without seemingly trying, I had passed every promotional exam available including the Part One and Two compulsory exam for a Non Commissioned Officer, and was promoted to senior unit sergeant within a further six months. Before I was fifteen years old, I had learnt to wear a uniform, march with and drill a squad of men, to field strip and fire the old .303 rifle and Bren machine gun. Fire a two inch mortar, strip a training hand grenade, fire a .38 calibre revolver, to successfully mount a raiding exercise against other units in an inter-service manoeuvers exercise, and to win the inter-service prize for the best unit in field craft.

Oh yes, if looked at in that light, I supoose I had quite a lot of experience . . . for a fourteen-year-old.

I closed the front of the machine and filled it with potatoes which began to beat themselves against the rough innards of the machine, ten minutes and they would be stripped of all skin. I turned back to the two young men, they had four years over me, it seemed so ridiculous . . . and yet . . . I felt it was my right.

'What exactly is it you want from me?'

They were just a little nervous, and understandably I suppose. They were about to let out a secret . . . and possession of that secret was dangerous. I knew both of them well, they were in the Army Cadet unit and I drilled them unmercifully every Tuesday and Thursday evening.

'Six of the inmates want to escape . . . to London.'

I blew out my cheeks involuntarily. Six . . . in one go, south to the capital city . . . without being caught. It had never been done. Within twelve hours three of them would be caught and they'd talk the moment the cell door was closed on them and the detectives made sure the screams couldn't be heard. Within thirty-six hours, most probably the rest would be caught. An escape on such a scale was bound to fail, the Police would be alerted, and every sniffer dog and detective would be mobilized to catch them. It couldn't be done . . . or could it?

Even someone as unlucky as myself has an ego, and I was, and still am, an eternal optimist. What was the difference between life and death, win or lose . . . an extremely thin line.

If it all went wrong, and it was proved I had been involved in the planning ... well ... it was back to the solitary confinement cell. I could feel the cold sweat coating my back at the thought of the padded cell, I tried not to show my nervousness. They had flattered me in the only way possible ... they had appealed to the unconventional thinker inside of me ... they had appealed to the piratical blood that I had inherited.

'All right. We'd better have a meeting here tonight. Let's say about 18.30. Bring along every one on the committee. It'll be safe here, because I am the only one who has the key, and anyway we can go up in the loft.'

They left without further word, and suddenly my heart beat crazily. I was jumping right into the fire ... if it was a trap and I was caught, six months extra time would be nothing to what would be handed down to me. But what did I have to lose, there was no one waiting outside for me. No mother ... father ... sister ... brother ... aunt ... uncle ... or grandparents. There were no girl friends ... school friends ... pets or enemies. There was just me and a remote possibility that one day I might be accepted into the Royal Marines.

For the rest of the day, I crept away from my garden digging duties and went up into the loft of the potato barn. I quickly rearranged some of the bales of straw which I used to keep the potatoes dry and cool, and brought along an old tin which could be used as an ashtray. We would have to sit in the dark when it came, and someone would have to keep a look out, just in case one of the screws was too conscientious in his duties. The hours dragged, and suddenly I realised that I didn't care whether I ended up in the solitary cell ... I had a purpose in life ... the boredom had been shattered.

They came into the potato shed singly, dodging around the shadows and into the door as fast as possible. When they were all collected upstairs there were six of them. Six out of a 120 or more represented the escape committee. And some of them were hostile to me.

'What's he got to do with this?'

I looked at the rough features and neanderthal habits of the person who'd spoken, he ruled by fear, but was also one of the oldest and longest serving inmates.

'We think he's got a lot to offer ... if any of you don't like the idea then we'll take a vote and then you can get out of the escape committee.'

So spoke the senior of seniors. Twenty years old, and serving a sentence for attempted murder of his father when he was fourteen years old. He was someone who was never argued with, unless someone was tired of living. Silence reigned. Cigarettes were lit and then the head of the committee spoke.

'There is an escape in the air. I've been asked if I can help.'

'What's so special about this escape which needs the entire escape group . . . and him?'

I looked to where the voice was coming from. Short and fat, and trying hard to grow a moustache to prove he was a man; Charlie White had a grudge against the world which led to three years for GBH. The leader of the group turned to face Charlie White, who became nervous with such attention.

'How many times have you been in solitary? How many beatings have you had in your life? And when was the last time you learnt anything? A long time ago, I should think, because you've learnt nothing up to now. You're out of the escape committee. Get out!'

Charlie White looked around him for support, but faces were turned away or looking at the floor. No one argued with the decision of the 'Boss'.

Silence soon settled after Charlie White had left, no one wanted to be thrown out of the escape committee, the status alone made life a lot easier in the school.

'Before we get down to business, is there anyone else here who feels like arguing?'

There was the emphatic shaking of heads.

'Good. What makes this escape different. Simple to answer. The sheer numbers of escapees. Six in total.' There were mutterings of astonishment and disbelief.

'Yes. I know. It's a big number. But these boys are determined to go. When they approached me, I tried to dissuade them from all going together. But their argument was the following: as they all come from the same place, Putney in London and surrounding area, the escape of one of them would bring down enough police in the area to mess it up for all of them. Which brings me to the reason why Dawson has been brought on to the escape committee.

You are to plan their escape from here to London. It will be taken over by one of the London members of the committee when they reach London. I want you to put together a plan that will get them away from here, and then into London. Have you got any ideas?'

My mind was in a whirl, how was I supposed to come up with answers so fast.

'When do they want to go?'

I needed time to think.

'They say they want to go in the next two weeks.'

I shook my head.

'No good. It's too damned cold. The distance alone, from here to the nearest railway station, would be enough to stop an army in this freezing weather. They have to wait at least four weeks until the temperatures reach well above freezing.'

'Why?'

I looked at the 'Boss' and could see he had a genuine interest.

'Wet feet. If the feet are wet and cold, the body is drained of it's internal heat faster than anything. Eight hours of that sort of thing and you can be sure at least two of them will drop out . . . fast. Second, if they go off now, and there is a snow storm, even the best plans can be thrown out of the window.'

'What's your recommendation?'

I lit another cigarette. It was prerogative of the escape committee, free tobacco, supplied by those requiring it's services.

'I would need to know the age of the escapees, what skills they have. Are they old enough to drive? Do they have any possibility of help from London? What financial resources they have access to, etc, etc. But most important is, what are they in here for? Serious crimes will bring down an army of police on their homes and relatives.'

'Are you saying then, if they have serious charge sheets against them, they should forget it?'

'No. But it will have to be taken into account in the planning. And should they get caught, then the next step for them will be borstal and locked doors, or even an adult prison, according to their age. What is important, is the motive for the escape?'

The 'Boss' was now sitting and watching me carefully.

'Explain yourself.'

I wondered why it was that I didn't keep my mouth shut, then at least I wouldn't get into situations like this. Why should I sort out other people's problems?

'What's the point of putting together an operation like this, just so they can go home and have a plate of beans and eggs whilst the police are surrounding the houses. Their parents and families are going to have the shock of their lives when their little Johny turns up at the back door, one step ahead of the police. Coleshill Approved School is a hell of a long way from Putney in London, in fact, far enough away for the police to put up a big cordon around Putney.'

'Normally we don't question the reason for the escape, it's a sort of unwritten law that an escapee gets whatever help he needs.'

I shrugged my shoulders. I was certain now that I had a big mouth. What the hell was wrong with an escape? Why should I worry about whether they get caught? The excitement was the most important thing. The blow at the establishment, that was important . . . There was no way I could believe what I was thinking.

'Six is a large number. It's important for the morale of this place that should the escape happen, then it should be a success. We should remove as many risks as possible . . . and who knows . . . perhaps we can claim some sort of record.'

And finally I had convinced myself, I would make it work.

'Ok. What do you need to know?'

No names. Ages, skills, charge sheets and the motives. What they have access to, and where they want to go.'

'Do you still stand by your insistence they don't go for at least four weeks?'

'Yes. One freezing cold night, and they've had it.'

'Ok. We meet again here in forty-eight hours. Can we use this place as a meeting place?'

'For as long as I'm on the potato detail, yes.'

It was the rule that all messages were passed between the parties by message carriers. None of the escape committee would ever meet the would-be escapees, thereby securing the identity of those whose job it was to help plan a successful escape. A successful escape was claimed when the escapee managed to carry out all the things which he set out to do. If

someone managed to go uncaptured for rather a long time, say
thirty days or so, then he broke a record. It was a rare event
when someone was never recaptured, and it happened only
twice in my time. So when an escape was planned, it also
carried the built-in factor of recapture and bringing back to
the same place of detention. The escape committee was fully
aware of the risks it worked under, but it knew that without
the efforts it made, there would be so many escapes that the
Government would be forced to change the security rating of
the place and then things would really become difficult.

We met forty-eight hours later in the loft of the potato barn,
each of us taking our places. The 'Boss' brought with him the
box of forty cigarettes which was the compulsory deposit paid
by anyone wanting to use the services of the committee. When
everyone was puffing away quite happily, the proceedings
began.

'We have the details you asked for, but I can't see what
good they'll be to you. Let's go down through the list, and
then we can ask questions afterwards. There are six escapees.
Ages range from fourteen to eighteen. Their charge sheets
range from stealing cars to breaking into the local sweet shop.
In fact, there's nothing exciting about them ... absolutely
nothing. There are a variety of reasons why they want to
escape, one of them being that the youngest hasn't heard from
home for twenty-eight days, and the oldest wants to go and lay
his girlfriend and kick her brother's teeth in. My opinion is,
that the youngest has the only valid reason for escaping.'

Destination Putney! As we said, they all come from the
Putney area.

What do they have access to? When they were questioned,
they came out with the usual bragging about big brothers who
were going to help them knock off a bank, to secret hoards of
money stashed away, and cars with the ignition keys in them
sitting in garages underneath the railway arches. Again, the
youngest was the most reasonable. He says the only thing he
has, is a mother who loves him and a stepfather who's hardly
ever at home ... and when he is ... he's pissed.

'So that's all of it. Now tell us what ideas are going through
your head.'

I scratched my head trying to pick up the key to the
problem. The more I thought about it, the more I realised

that he was right ... there was hardly any reason for one of them to escape ... except for the youngest ... whoever he was.

'The one who's got problems at home, the fourteen-year-old, how long has he got to serve?'

'Three years!'

Everyone was surprised ... except perhaps myself.

'What did he do? Rob a bank?'

'No ... He threw a brick through a jewellers window and stole a watch for his mother's birthday. When he ran off, he left over 14,000 quids worth of jewellery in the window, which, someone else came along and helped themselves to.'

'Is that what he says?'

The boss looked at me, and I could feel a certain personal interest of his behalf. he knew far more about this young boy then he was letting on.

'It's what I know.'

He didn't leave any room for argument. I'd been asked for my ideas and not a personal judgement.

'Ok. The numbers are too big. Six escapees. By the time that reaches the press, the six escapees will be six desperate men, armed and dangerous. Why don't we cut it down and do it in stages. Two, two, and two?' He shook his head.

'No, If one goes, they all go.'

I had the distinct feeling there was more to this escape than met the eye. But there was no way I could voice my opinion on it. The 'Boss' ... was the boss.

'Good. Can any of them drive ... legally?'

'Two of them. But they had their licenses taken away. Stealing cars.'

Suddenly my head was clear enough to think, and it did so, at high speed.

'As far as I can see, the purpose of this escape is to get one person to London. That person must be the fourteen-year-old. Ok. He can't drive, so he would need a driver and an escort because he can't walk the streets alone. Too suspicious. Can't go by train unless we can obtain train tickets ... legally ... and then it's risky if the railway police are after them. It's too dangerous to hitch hike, and we don't know any family member who would even risk the danger of coming to pick them up with a car or truck. It's my feeling that the other three are just to provide flak to cover the true purpose of this escape. Their job is to keep the Police busy whilst the fourteen-year-old is doing something else.'

The Boss looked at me, and I wished I'd kept my big mouth shut. There were some things which were not supposed to be uttered in public, and I'd uttered one of them. He curtly nodded his head in the direction of the door, and the rest of the committee quickly went down the wooden stairs to wait to be called back. Only I was left sitting on the floor next to the 'Boss'. He studied me with cold eyes, and then slowly lit another cigarette.

'I wish you hadn't said that.'

So did I.

'This will be your last job for the escape committee.'

I looked at the cigarettes in the box, perhaps that was the penalty for being too sure of one's self.

'Sorry.'

He shrugged his shoulders and pushed the cigarette box towards me with his foot. I took one and lit it.

'The fourteen-year-old is my cousin. It's been kept a secret from the authorities because it's not allowed to have family members serving time in the same prison. I'm due to leave in three months, but I can't leave until some unfinished business is taken care of in London. It's so important to me to settle this business before I go out, that I'm prepared to get my sentence extended by a month.'

I took a deep breath and let it out slowly. That was desperate measures.

'My cousin is the only one who can take care of the problems. Two of the others are going with him for protection, and as you said, the other three are for diversion purposes. How did you find out?'

I was sure he wouldn't believe me.

'Intuition.'

'That's a hell of a thing to say. But I believe you.'

'What do you really need me for? If this business is so important for you, I'm sure you can come up with the necessary to do the job.'

'I could. But then, once the police start to capture them, the questions will be asked and somehow or other someone is going to put two and two together. This has got to be done without any connections to me, or any of mine. You're supposed to be a good planner, then plan.'

'How long is your cousin supposed to stay free?'

'He needs thirty-six hours in London.'

'You know that having him arrested by the police is a big risk. Someone could intervene and have him sent somewhere else before you get the information you need, which is what I assume you're after.'

'What do you suggest?'

'If we can get him to London . . . then we can get him back here.'

'You mean he goes out . . . and comes back, and then gives himself up to the Governor? And how does he explain the time in between.'

'He stayed hidden in the barn on the school farm.'

'But it could take a week for him to get to London and back.'

'No. You say he needs thirty-six hours in London. Good. By car from here to London, is about five hours. Then another five hours back. He needs only forty-eight hours, let's say sixty hours. Agreed.'

He nodded his head, warily.

'Two and a half days. That's a time which could be explained away in the school farm, if someone were to break into the school kitchens and steal some food, say, after thirty-six hours. What we need is a vehicle and driver. And not just any driver. We need someone who is level headed, doesn't take risks, and can complete a journey of some 500 miles.'

Suddenly he was sat upright.

'Who?'

'The Irishman.'

'Donovan?'

'Yes.'

A smile creased his face.

'But of course. Why didn't I think of that . . .'

Suddenly his face dropped.

'. . . but he's not in the market for escaping.'

'200 Senior Service cigarettes, and you've got yourself a car and driver. You'll need to send him out twenty-four hours before your cousin is due to leave, to give him time to get a car and fuel. Donovan is in for Her Majesty's Pleasure. He's got nothing to lose, the next stop is a closed prison. He could get out and in and say he stayed in the barn. The only thing that will do for his reputation is to confuse things and make him look a bit soft. Something he can remedy with the next fight.'

'And what if he decides to do a bunk in London, then my cousin is stranded in the city.

'That's a risk you have to take . . . unless you take him yourself. You said you were prepared to stay another month.'

'An escape for me would be the most suspicious thing ever. I've been here for five years . . . five long years, if I were to escape now . . . I and all mine would be investigated until they knew how many hairs there would be up my backside. Then I would be straight into a closed prison and another five years.'

'What the hell did you do to get five years here?'

'Arson. I burnt down a house. There was an old woman living in the cellar . . . a tramp . . . she died in the fire. I was twelve months in a closed detention centre with no privileges, then they moved me out here.'

'Why did you burn the house down?'

The eyes were dark brown, and held me prisoner for a long time, finally the decision was made. He spoke quietly and slowly . . . as if to ensure I didn't misunderstand anything.

'I was hiding some money I'd stolen from a Post Office, when I saw this tramp watching me from the cellar . . . she was watching me with the unblinking eyes of those who've already seen too much. She frightened me . . . badly. I fired the house because she'd frightened me and because I couldn't forget those eyes . . . I'd known all the time she was still in there. When I came before the court, I told them I'd been looking for something to steal in the house and then set it on fire because there was nothing there. In the end they believed me . . . but I still see those eyes . . . even now.'

I sat on the old wooden floor, dust surrounding me, and an indescribable silence filled the air. He was serving time for manslaughter. And now he'd told me everything. Suddenly muffled voices came from below.

'Heh, come on. It's nearly bed time. We have to get back before the last roll call.'

I looked across at the old face on the young shoulders and

saw the longing for peace in the eyes.

'Talk to Donovan for me, Dawson. He can have his cigarettes. Set the whole thing up, and leave me out of it. If my cousin comes back and he's been able to do what I needed, then good. If anything goes wrong, and I need to stay here for extra time, then I'll have to work someone over so that I get an extra month. If anything does go wrong, then I'll be looking for you.'

As he got up he kicked the cigarettes across to me.

'Take them with you. Use them to bait Donovan. You just tell me when and how.'

Then he was gone, and I was left to lock the place up and find my way back to the school buildings in the dark. I wished I'd never seen this place, this thing was one number too big for me.

It was during the Sunday morning march to church two weeks later, that Donovan disappeared. As was the custom, come rain, wind, shine or arctic storm . . . we were forced to march the four miles there and back to church. We marched in columns of three, thirty to a block, very often bent over against the winds or driving rains, and herded by the wardens. The only thing which was missing were the chains to keep us together. Donovan disappeared immediately after the church service whilst we were marching back . . . and I held my breath for the first hour. By four o'clock that afternoon I began to take a few deep breaths, Donovan must have made it. The only thing which worried me, was the fact that Donovan hated missing his meals. Somehow, from somewhere, Donovan had to get food. That was the only weak link in the plan.

At midnight thirty on the following day, six of the inmates ran across a moonlit, frozen, cricket field and disappeared into the hedges which line the roads to Coleshill. None of them saw one of their number detach itself and go in another direction. And none of them heard the engine of the car which crept quietly down the silent lanes towards its own destination.

On the following Thursday morning, two ravenously hungry and dishevelled escapees where found in the hay barn of the school farm by one of the supervising wardens. Donovan, the happy-go-lucky Irishman was placed in solitary confinement and then shipped to a more secure establishment. The fourteen-year-old cousin, was given twelve of the best from the Governor and then stripped of all privileges for three months. His escape was not taken seriously which was why he wasn't put into solitary confinement. Whatever his trip to London had been about, it must have been a success, because thirty days later the senior boy was quietly released into the freedom of the world.

Of the others who escaped, came one of the greatest mysteries. Four were recaptured within forty-eight hours of each other, they'd been seen moving through the streets of Putney and were captured when they'd stopped to go into a betting shop. The shop was owned by one of the fathers.

But it was the fifth member who turned out to be the dark horse. He was never recaptured, and his file was never reclaimed from the Governor's office by the police or any other organisation. He had effectively disappeared from the face of the earth. His disappearance caused immense speculation amongst the inmates, even to the point where some said he'd gone abroad, but it also provided the lifeblood which the place lived on. It was these escapes which fired the imagination of all those who were kept there, and it was these escapes which prevented those who were kept there from slowly dying inside themsleves. It was these blows against the establishment, which made an otherwise sombre people . . . smile.

The cold of winter gave way to the warm spring days which made the buds on the trees burst out into all shades of green. Birds built nests in the high roofs, the cows on the school farm calved. The gardens were dug and plants planted, and three of the inmates were taken to a hospital in Birmingham, with a rare 'flu. There were more than sixty of the school population laid down in a makeshift sick ward on the second floor. They were ill . . . and how.

One was forced to walk around the buildings with handkerchiefs over the mouths to help stem the stink from above, until one day the Governor closed off the main part of the building and forced the healthy ones into other dormitories. It totally destroyed the routine of the place, something which none of us were sorry about, as so many of the healthy ones were required to help feed and clean those who were sick. Beds had to be changed every twelve hours, because of sweating and urine, and three times a day food had to be distributed.

The matron and deputy matron were already at their wit's
end, and the doctors were spending more time at the school
trying to stem the flow of those who were falling sick. The
Governor was forced to bring in outside nursing staff from one
of the prison hospitals and forbid the rest of us to get
anywhere near this part of the building. It took six weeks, and
what was suspiciously like two deaths before the epidemic was
under control. In respect of the two suspected deaths, there is
only speculation. But . . . two of the three who were taken into
Birmingham City Hospital never ever returned, and one day
one of the warders was seen to be packing the private
belongings from their lockers. In such a society the simplest of
actions will bring forth a welter of speculation, and experience
dictates that most of the speculation is correct.

It was the Governor who moved quickly to stop the
rumours, and his action was sufficient to confirm what we had
been thinking. He said that the two had been transferred to a
place nearer their homes because of their sickness and pressure
from the parents. Such patent lies were unworthy of the
Governor, we knew he didn't have a heart and certainly not
one that could be bent by any parent, the man was ice cold.

Spring ran into summer, and I was forced to play cricket
and football every Saturday and Sunday. The former I was
always happy to watch from the sidelines, and the latter I
hated with a vengeance. Anybody and everybody who fancied
himself to be a great footballer, would show off his prowess
with the ball to the undying adulation of his followers.

Football was, and is, a game for mass hysteria and crowd
control. And there was no way I could bring myself to curse
and scream and shout at the antics of twenty-two Prima
Donnas who were trying to dribble a ball across a field.

Though it must be admitted that I was not totally immune
to the lure of the leather ball. My sport, and one which I
revelled in . . . was rugby. The game of gentlemen . . . played
for gentlemen . . . by gentlemen. It is a game for which one
expects not to give any mercy and also not to receive any. It is
a game for which persons like myself were aptly suited. We
lived in a society which was close to the border between the
untamed animal world and the so called civilised world, our
values were different, and rightly so. When you took possession
of the ball, you knew there was twelve others behind you who

were going to try and take it . . . with force. There was only
one rule to be followed, biting was not allowed. Otherwise it
was every man for himself. I felt at home with this game, and
it was no wonder in the end when our team was forced to stop
playing against the normal civilian teams, there were too many
complaints about hard, dangerous, and injurious play. What
the other teams didn't realise, was that we knew no other way,
we were a product of the way we were forced to live. In our
society one rose and fell according to one's ability to survive,
and in our society there were no places for the faint-hearted.

And then one day something happened. I was called to the
Governor's office. I was kept waiting for perhaps just a few
minutes, so, as the school code of conduct goes, it was a good
sign. I wasn't in trouble.

When I marched into the office and gave my name, I saw
that Len Newman was standing in the corner. Now, between
Len Newman and myself the wounds had been healed, but
things had never been the same again. I had learnt not to trust
anyone, not even him, and now that I saw him standing there
behind the Governor my instincts said to watch him.

The Governor sat back in his chair and took a good look at
me.

'You've changed a lot, Dawson. You're bigger and stronger,
and I understand you have a lot of respect amongst your
contemporaries.

One did not answer the Governor unless a specific question
was asked. I waited for him to continue, it seemed to take
forever.

'What are your plans for the future?'

For the future! I hadn't even bothered to think about it
anymore.

'I'm . . . I'm not really sure, sir. Well . . . what I mean to
say . . . is . . . I haven't thought about it anymore, sir.'

The fingers were steepled below his chin. Somehow he was
enjoying this.

'You're due for release next year. In fact, in nine months
time, you are to go out into the wide world and face it. I think
it's about time you thought about your future . . . and
seriously. Mr Newman tells me that when you first came into
the school, you had plans to join the Royal Marines and to
become a Commando. What's happened to those ideas?'

I looked across to Len Newman, who stood watching me
. . . impassively. The ball was in my court.

'Well, sir. The thing is . . . I'd given up the idea of going
into the Royal Marines after the last bout of solitary
confinement. I was left with the impression that my chances of
getting into the service . . . were non existent.'

He looked embarrassed.

'That's in the past, and I hope you'll forget it. What is
important is the future, your future. I want you to go away
and think about what you want to do. When you're sure about
it you can go to Mr Newman and talk with him about it. Mr
Newman is interested in helping you in any way he can. Any
questions?'

'No, sir.'

It was the stock answer to a stock question. Neither side
expected the other to change the rules of the game.

7

It was a sunny day, and I'd finished a back breaking morning digging the heavy black soil which represented the life and soul of the gardening department. I had just passed my examinations in Horticultural Botany, Soils and Manures, and was the not-so-proud possessor of said document issued by the Union Of Educational Institutes. I was almost too tired to face the walk back to the school buildings, and a lunch which was going to weigh in my stomach like a brick.

The dining room was silent except for the sounds of cutlery being banged against the heavy prison plates. Nobody had the energy to talk or even lift his head to see what his neighbour was up to. The food was consumed mechanically, whilst the meagre rations of tap water which was served in a metal jug, were drunk sparingly. Each person was more concerned with facing the coming afternoon's heat in their respective jobs; whether it was farming, gardening or building the new house for the Governor, it was going to be hard work. The mail call was a quiet affair with the warden going around giving the letters to the individuals as they ate. When he stopped at our table, I didn't even bother to look up. After all, in more than two years I'd never once received a letter.

'Dawson. You've got a letter.'

The shock must have registered on my face.

'Close your mouth, Dawson. And take your letter.'

They hadn't even bothered to open the letter. It was an official letter. I was frightened to open it, because I knew once it was open there was no turning back. The outside world was calling, and I was frightened to death of it. I tried to leave the letter on the table as if I'd forgotten it, but when I rose from the table to leave the dining room one of the others chased after me.

'Heh, Cannonball, you've forgotten your letter.'

Cannonball was my nickname, given to me after a certain rugby game where it was said I'd devastated the opposition like a cannonball.

I took the letter but didn't want to open it. I carried it everywhere I went until I was suddenly confronted by Len Newman as I walked towards the potting sheds.

'What does the letter say?'

He obviously knew where the letter had come from and was waiting for me to tell him. I waved my hands around like some rubber doll, and shrugged my shoulders.

'I haven't opened it yet.'

'Why don't you open it?'

'Jahh, perhaps I'll do it a bit later.'

'You're scared of the letter.'

I protested my innocence, but he was absolutely right. He took the letter from my grubby hand and opened it. He studied the contents for a minute and then read it out.

'It's from the Ministry of Defence . . .'

Even I knew that, it was in large black letters on the front of the envelope.

'. . . The Royal Marines recruiting office. They thank you for your letter asking for recruiting pamphlets, and enclose them herein.'

It would be embarrasing to see a picture of myself as I was at this moment, I was a picture of nonchalant innocence.

'Huh. I never ever sent a letter to anyone.'

'Yes, you did. I even posted it.

'Huh.'

'You're repeating yourself.'

He thrust the large envelope back into my hands and walked off. There was no turning back, Pandora's box had been opened.

I studied the contents of this envelope night and day. For hours I would sit and look at my hand written name on the envelope and wonder if the person who had written it, knew about me. I didn't know what was expected of me in the outside world, I didn't even know anything about it. Out there were a million eyes watching everything you did, but here . . .

here there were but a few. Here, it was not necessary to hide your personal feelings, but out there . . . Here, you knew the consequences of straying into someone's own private and personal territory, but out there . . . Here, I didn't need money, but out there . . . Here, I knew who my friends and enemies were, but out there . . . there were no friends. In this place, black was black and white was white, but out there . . . there were all shades of grey according to the dictates of the one who used the colours.

I was frightened. Frightened because I was sure the world would see me as some sort of monster who had escaped from behind his steel bars.

I'd listened to some of the horrific stories from those who'd been returned to the school. Stories of how they'd been treated outside, how the world had turned their backs on them. They had committed crimes again, just to be put back into the safety of an approved school. Here, in this place, I knew what and who I was, nobody passed judgement on me and nobody expected me to perform like some circus animal for them. Here . . . I was me . . . out there . . . I could only be what they would allow me to be. If they threw the crumbs on the floor and told me to eat . . . I was in no position to argue with them.

It took a lot of courage to talk to Len Newman. Because I was talking about my future, suddenly it was down to me to make the decisions, the first time in my entire life. We stood in the potting sheds looking out over the gardens. He handed me a cigarette and then lit it.

'Well. What's your decision?'

'I don't know. What will it be like in the Royal Marines? The pamphlets are full of nice pictures, but it doesn't say what it's like.'

'It's hard. Bloody hard. The regimen is not as strict as here, with the emphasis on self governing. But, don't kid yourself as to what is required of you. They will demand your soul, and the breath in your body, but, if you can complete the course and are awarded the 'Green Beret' of the Commando forces, then you can be damned sure you have earned it. You will be one of a rare breed, and will have the right to face the world on your own terms.'

'What happens if I agree. What I mean . . .'

Of course I'd made up my mind, it was clear, but my experiences made me wary. I wanted someone to tell me the facts . . . and not some public relations bullshit . . . but I had to find the right words which would trigger that store of information in Len Newman's head. I was struggling with myself . . . what did he need to trigger that memory of his.

'You are the only one who can tell me what I would be facing if I join the Royal Marines. I have to trust that what you tell me is the truth.'

The words got home. I had hit the nail on the head. It took more than two hours, but he talked and talked, and at the end of it I knew what I was going to do.

'So. What's your decision?'

'I'll join.'

'That's not so easy. You don't join, they invite you to join them. You'll have to sit a lot of tests, and go through a very strict medical examination. It will be hard and nerve wracking, the waiting is what kills you. The waiting for an answer. The Yes or No, to your future. That is what is going to be the hardest. Can you do it? Six months you'll have to wait, before you know the answer . . . and in that six months you cannot afford to have any problems here. I will not be able to help you . . . you'll be on your own the moment you decide to go ahead.'

'Do you think I have the necessary qualifications to get in?'

'From what I know about you . . . I think you have. Though I must admit the qualifications required will be of a higher standard than when I was in the service. You'll have to do a lot of work brushing up all your educational knowledge, but that is something I could arrange here. I would suggest you think about it for twenty four hours, and then let me know.'

I went away, and thought, and thought and thought about it. And the more I thought about what sort of future I had ahead of me, the more I came to realise that joining the service was the only future I had. When I saw Len Newman the following day, he stood silently in front of me and waited for my answer.

'I'll join the Royal Marines, if they'll have me.'

He just nodded his head, I guessed he'd known the answer all along.

'Good. Then let's start right now. From now on, you have to avoid trouble like the plague. You cannot afford to get mixed up in any fights, you cannot afford to antagonise any of the wardens. You must learn to be five minutes early no matter where you are going or what you're doing. And you must turn in excellent work no matter how much you may hate what you're doing. You must learn to be military clean and tidy and keep your personal items in order. You should learn to keep your boots and shoes spotlessly clean at all times and any tools or equipment you use you should look after as if your life depended on them. From now on you should think and behave like a soldier, and like a grown man. Give up all the petty arguments and back stabbing, and don't let yourself be provoked into a fight. There will be certain persons here, who, once they know that you're trying for the service will try and ruin your chances. Don't let them get at you, avoid them, walk away, no matter how much you'd like to hammer them. Your chances of getting into the service will depend on the character report which is sent from here. From now on you'll have to work twice as hard as anyone else here if you want to achieve the impossible . . . and what you want, is asking for the impossible.'

I nodded my head and thought about the prospects of keeping out of trouble. That seemed about as impossible as joining the Royal Marines.

'Will not the fact that I'm in an approved school reduce my chances of getting into the service?'

'No. Your file states that you are here because of the difficulties you experienced with your foster parents, and because the children's department were unable to place you in a home. You were too old for adoption, and the children's department had no place where a child of your age could be placed. There was no alternative but to put you into the care of an Approved School until you reached the age to be able to look after yourself.'

'When I'm asked about my parents, what shall I say?'

'You just say what's on your file. They're dead.'

For a moment I thought about the parents I didn't have . . . or at least the ones everyone was trying hard to convince me I didn't have, and decided to drop the subject immediately . . . it was only going to cause trouble and as Len Newman had said, I didn't need any more trouble.

'What do I have to do now? What I mean is, what is the next step?'

'You don't have to do anything. I'll go and see the Governor in a few minutes and tell him of your decision. He will then have to submit a request to the governing board asking their permission for you to apply to join the Royal Marines. It is not a foregone conclusion that you will be able to apply, someone could quite easily decide against it and then you would have to forget the idea; at least for as long as you are in this place, I would like you to know that I will put my recommendation behind your application.'

And true to his word, he did. Then began the awful waiting, the not knowing whether or not my application would be accepted. Fourteen days later I was called to the Governor's office and told that I had been granted permission to apply. I felt such relief, that for some days I felt as though I was walking on air. The first big hurdle had been crossed.

Len Newman made the application on my behalf, and again I waited. Each day at mail call I sat on the edge of my seat hoping to have my name read out, and each day my hopes were dashed. I was becoming more nervous every day, trying to control the emotions running through me. It took more than a month before the day came that a buff coloured envelope arrived from the Royal Marines recruiting office in Birmingham. They were inviting me to attend their offices to fill out the application forms and to sit a general examination. From that day on, I went through the school routine like someone in a dream. I neither saw, nor realised, what I was doing anymore. I could only count the days, the hours and the minutes until the day arrived for me to attend the examination.

When the time came, I was informed by the Governor that Len Newman had asked permission to take me there. We departed at eight-thirty in the morning, and I was a bag of nerves. This day was to be a very decisive day in my life, and being aware of this fact didn't help me to calm down. I was painfully aware of the fact that I was on my own, and that if I failed, then there was only myself to blame.

For weeks I'd been attending lessons given by one warden or the other in Maths, English, History and general knowledge. And as each day had gone by, it only served to bring home the fact that my educational abilities were abysmal. I cursed and worried my way through one examination after another, until I thought I could never pass the enrolment exam.

When I sat in the examination room with twenty other young men, I could feel the difference in our status. I was the convict sitting with twenty others who came from normal homes and had normal lives. This was my first taste of the outside world, and every time one of them looked at me I could feel my prison number burning it's mark into my forehead. The fact that we were all there for one common purpose, did nothing to allay the chasm which separated me from them. They had an enormous advantage over me, and I somehow couldn't dismiss the thought. When I looked down at the examination paper in front of me, I felt myself sliding into a panic . . . there was no way I could pass this examination and prove myself to be worthy of being chosen to join the Royal Marines . . . not me . . . the convict. How could I be chosen from amongst twenty other normal and decent young men. I could feel the mantle of the convict covering me, and I was sure that everyone there could also see it.

Len Newman brought me back to the school in the late afternoon, and I was never so glad to get back. I felt as though I was back amongst my own kind, and I realised that I'd never been so scared before. The outside world was not a place for me.

I tried to convince myself that I'd failed the test, that I wouldn't have to go out into that world outside and face it. And on the journey back I hadn't even been able to talk about what had happened, I was ashamed of myself and what I was. I had convinced myself I was something better than I truly was, and had paid the price for such stupidity.

Days ran into weeks, the summer became hotter, and I immersed myself in the school's routine. There were the usual Sunday marches to church, the football matches every Saturday, a rugby match on Wednesdays. I worked in the school gardens until the sweat ran off my back, and I fulfilled my role as sergeant of the school's Army Cadet force. I wandered the halls of the place aimlessly, unable to concentrate on anthing, painfully waiting for the letter that would tell me I had failed.

Then I was called to the Governor's office.

When I saw Len Newman standing there in the office, I knew that it could only be bad news, and I felt sorry that I'd ever involved him in this thing. It was the Governor who spoke to me.

'So, Dawson.'

'Yes, sir.'

I could feel my heart hammering in my chest, and I wished to God he would get it over with.

'I have a letter for you from the Ministry of Defence in London, It is from the Royal Marines, You're invited to join the service on the fifth of January next year.'

I wanted to cry, I wanted to scream, I wanted to die, and I wanted to laugh. But most of all I wanted to be alone. I hardly heard the rest of what he said because my world was spinning.

'I want to congratulate you on your achievement. Excellent. You are a credit to the school. Never before have we had someone who has been able to overcome such difficulties and to achieve such remarkable results. I would like you to know that we, that is all of us, are very proud of you. Because of your situation, you will stay here at the school until next year, and will be released on January the fifth. From here you will take a train to Deal in Kent where you will join the training depot of the Royal Marines . . . Well done.'

One month before my departure from the school, a civilian tailor was brought in and I was measured for some clothes. I was allowed to choose the material for the suits that were made for me, and also to choose my footwear.

I hardly noticed the excitement that was in the air as Christmas arrived, and plans were being made for the Christmas parole. I no longer felt part of the establishment, I lived in another world, a very sad and lonely one. I listened to the laughter and the curses, the moaning and the groaning. I listened to the plans which were being made about what each of them would do over Christmas, and yet I was no part of it. The words and the people swam around me in a grey mist.

Instead I listened to the ticking of the clock, and as each tick sounded I knew I was drawing nearer to the day that I would leave this world and join one which was so different. I watched the world that had become so familiar to me, drop it's mantle of sunshine and green grasses and take on the cold grey cloak of winter. I was painfully aware of the changing season as the leaves fell from the trees and the cold grey fogs filled the air. I saw every minute detail which passed before my eyes, details which told me of my life in this place.

When the school was finally empty and again I was the only one in it, I walked the silent corridors remembering all the things which had taken place in one corner or the other. I relived the memories, both good and bad. I sat for a long time in the solitary confinement cell, it's door now wide open, and remembered the tears I'd shed there. I walked the gardens I had tended, now covered in frost and grey mist. I spent hours sitting in the potato shed I'd worked in for so long, and I looked at the ground I had so often dug over.

I walked alone along the route we had taken so often on our marches to church, reliving the plans we'd made for our sudden escapes. I listened to the voices which accompanied me, and wished they were still there. I walked and walked in my world of loneliness, turning my head expecting to see one of them there, and seeing only the emptiness of a freezing cold path.

I couldn't listen to the Christmas carols on the radio which the solitary warden listened to, because it reminded me of the world I would never see. I became lost in the cold silent mists which surrounded the school and watched the lights of Christmas behind the windows of the houses. I lived and died a thousand times during that last Christmas, shedding the bonds which held me fast to the life I had lived. I remembered my life in the foster home, the shouting and the beatings, the sounds of children's voices in the late evening sun. But most of all, I asked myself, from where have I come, and where am I going to?

Postscript

It would be unfair to the reader if I did not finish this story without describing how my life finally unfolded.

As I've said, I always had the feeling that my parents were still alive, and it was inevitable, I suppose, that in the end I would try to find them.

My search started with my mother, whom I found alive and well through the help of the Royal Marines. After months of searching through Government archives at Somerset House in London (the home of all births, deaths, and marriage registrations) I came across the details of my birth. Included in the details was the name and address of my mother. Further exhaustive searches revealed that she hadn't died and that she was living and working in the house of the Austin family in Edgbaston, Birmingham, as housekeeper.

It took me many weeks to pluck up the courage to write to her and announce that her son was alive and well. I followed this up with a telephone call to the house and arranged a meeting with her.

When I met her, I met a woman whom I'd dreamed of having as a mother. She was small, dark haired, and very slim, a lively woman, who hid well the harshness that she had been subjected to.

We talked for nearly two hours about our lives and what had happened to each other, to discover that a web of lies had been spun by members of the Birmingham City children's department to prevent her from ever finding me.

After she had left the Castle Bromwich Hospital, she had made strenuous efforts to find me, only to be told that I had been adopted and that she had no parental rights anymore.

She then went on to tell me about my father, and gave me his full name and service rank when he was in the air force. From this information I was able to go to the Ministry of Defence and find out where my father had been, and still was living.

When I went to my father's house near Tunbridge Wells, he refused to admit that I was his son until I signed a paper saying that I would never ever make any claims against his estate. Then he asked me never to come to his house again, something which I could easily do.

The contact with my mother was broken due to my long stays abroad and I never saw her again. It took another twenty years before I was able to contact her again because of bureaucratic changes within England. It wasn't until I made contact with the Birmingham City Council in January of 1988 that they were able to tell me more details about my life. The most important detail being that I had a sister who was born eighteen months after me.

In the intervening twenty years many things have happened to me, the least of these events being that I was married and had two children.

The saddening facts of this unfortunate marriage are that my daughter Susan Nicola died of a tumour on the brain when she was nearly three years of age; and my son Christopher John was removed to a foster home after it was discovered his mother had been mistreating him during my absence.

Whilst in the foster home on a North Devon farm, my son was involved in a tragic accident when his right foot was cut off by a grass cutting machine. Only due to the dedicated efforts of two police officers, and the staff of the Barnstaple Hospital, was my son's foot sewn back on to the leg. He is crippled for life, perhaps not only physically but mentally by the experiences that have befallen him. It was at this point that I realised I had failed badly to look after my son, and had been unable to offer him the protection that a father should. I felt I no longer had the right to interfere in his life and stepped back to allow those better able to look after him, to do so. I have not seen him for more than twelve years and doubt seriously if he would ever want to see me.

In February 1988, I wrote a letter to my mother, which she

answered immediately. This time the contact will not be broken.

In July 1988, a friend went to see my mother and took some photographs of her. She is now sixty-four years old, a very lively and happy woman who still lives in Edgbaston. I am in the process of making an audio cassette for her, which will be our means of communication.

My father? He died in April of 1987 at the age of eighty-seven. I can only wonder what his last thoughts were for the life he had led, and also wonder if he ever spared a thought for the two illegitimate children that he brought into the world. My mother was able to verbally confirm that my sister was also his child, conceived on one of his weekend visits to his parents' house where my mother was working as housekeeper. She had loved him passionately, and had been willing to cover his indiscretions.

My sister, Jean, will probably never know of my existence, because of the strict rules of adoption. But should she one day want to find out where she comes from, then there will be a reference on her files that she has a brother living as a writer in West Germany.

I ask for my mother's forgiveness for what I have written about her in this book. Whatever the rights and wrongs of what she did, she is still my mother, and I hope this book will fill in many gaps which she surely has about what happened to her son.

I would also like to thank the memory of a man who eventually became a true friend and mentor. He risked everything to help me get where I wanted. A better friend I could not have asked for in Len Newman.

To Sheila Ann Summers, wherever she may be, I would like to give a special thank you for the friendship she gave me at a most critical time in my life.

And to all those who have helped shape my life, both good and bad, I thank you for the experience of knowing you.

G.D. Dawson.
September 1988.